WE'RE GETTING DIVORCED

AN INSIDER'S GUIDE THROUGH THE DIVORCE PROCESS

BY ZACHARY SMITH

Edited by Regan Smith and Megan Kelly
Cover Art by Leah Perzichilli

To my wife, Mindy, for her love and support throughout the process of writing this book, and for hopefully having a sense of humor about a book on divorce being dedicated to her.

Table of Contents

Introduction

In my time as a family law attorney, I have met hundreds, maybe even thousands, of people going through difficult divorces, custody disputes, adoptions and other stressful situations. Most people are in full "crisis mode" by the time they make it to my office, and are usually scared, confused, and want to know what to expect going forward. One of the most calming things I can do is to provide an education as to the relevant law, court procedure, and "unwritten rules" that will come in to play. I know that when I have a problem in my life – if I'm sick or my car is making a funny noise, the first thing I do is find out more about what is going on. If my doctor tells me that I need my tonsils removed, I would seek out more information about what that entails, what recovery time is, what tonsils do, what flavor of ice cream is best for recovery, and so on. Call me a control freak, but the more knowledge I have about a situation, the better equipped I feel that I am to handle it.

That being said, even if I have done enough research to be the world foremost tonsil expert, it's probably not a good idea for me to break out the pliers and Swiss army knife and get to work on my own. Likewise, this book wasn't written with the intention to replace the need to work with an attorney for your divorce or custody case, it is more of a supplement to help you work with your attorney and have a better understanding of what they are doing. The great (and often challenging) part about practicing family law is that there are really no two situations that are exactly alike. It would be impossible to put together a book that would guide everyone through the law as it relates to every situation that could possibly arise, especially as new situations arise every day that have never been dealt with in the past.

So if this is not a do-it-yourself manual, and you'll still need an attorney after reading this book, what's the point? First, I'm hoping it'll be at least fairly entertaining, or at least as entertaining as a book about divorce and custody law can be. Second, I've always wanted to be a published author, and this book paves the way for introducing that crime drama I've been secretly working on late nights. Most importantly, I want people who are going through a divorce or custody battle to have a resource to turn to that is informative, easy to read, more reliable than the mis-information vault known as the internet, and convenient. Forgiving my tendency to make constant car comparisons and awkward pop-culture references, I hope you'll find this book to be a helpful resource if you, or someone you know, is going through a family law controversy.

Lastly, as the inevitable disclaimer that must come with anything ever touched by an attorney, I do need to point out what should be obvious – this book is not specific legal advice for any particular person's situation. Everyone's facts are unique, laws change all the time, and situations vary from county to county, state to state, and person to person. This book should not be used as a substitute for competent legal advice in any way, and is not to be construed as providing legal advice to help you or anyone else work through the legal system.

PART ONE
Chapter One

The Choice is Yours: You choose how much your divorce costs.

What would you say if I asked you to tell me the biggest factor in determining the total cost of your divorce? Would you say the assets at stake? Your attorney's hourly rate? Whether or not your soon-to-be-ex decides to wake up on the wrong side of the bed every morning? Nice try, but unfortunately you're a bit off-base. Contrary to popular belief, the answer to this question is actually quite simple. The biggest factor in determining the total cost of your divorce is—drum roll please—*you*.

The average cost of a divorce in the US is somewhere between five thousand and ten thousand dollars. In my practice, I've had clients rack up as little as fifteen hundred dollars and as much as thirty-five thousand dollars in legal fees. The difference between a four thousand dollar divorce and a forty thousand dollar divorce is almost always the client's attitude towards their ex. Those clients who walk into my office with a courteous relationship and an ability to amicably resolve differences walk out with a smaller bill, and those clients on the opposite end tend to walk out with a sore wallet. That's not to say that the latter client is a combative person or is doing something wrong; it usually just means that they happen to have issues with their ex that can't be resolved through simple negotiation.

Even though the modern family court system is set up to encourage mediation, negotiation, and working together, there will still be circumstances when parties can't agree and a judge or arbitrator needs to step in and make a final decision. But before you decide to duke it out in the courtroom, make sure to undergo a cost-benefit analysis to ensure you're making a financially sensible move.

A particularly ugly divorce I handled a few years ago

illustrates how easily a four thousand dollar divorce can escalate into a forty thousand dollar nightmare. On the surface, the divorcing couple didn't appear to have much that couldn't easily be resolved--they didn't have children, the house and vehicles weren't at issue, and there was no multimillion dollar fortune to spar over.   Despite the cost it incurred, both parties insisted on making every minor detail a major issue because they were so upset with each other.

   At one point during the divorce I got a call from the wife, who I was representing. She was furious that the husband insisted on keeping the downstairs sofa. I asked her how much she thought the sofa was worth, and she told me she thought it was around three hundred fifty dollars. I had seen a picture of it and thought fifty dollars would have been generous, but that's beside the point. I told her that bringing a motion in court and attending a hearing to discuss the couch would cost roughly two thousand dollars and asked if she felt this couch was worth it. She had already gotten the higher quality upstairs furniture and this was the last remaining unresolved issue.

   However, she told me it wasn't so much about the cash as it was the principle. She was set on "winning," whatever that meant to her. My recommendation was to take the two thousand dollars she would otherwise use on legal fees and buy a really nice new couch instead. And if that wasn't enough of a "win," she could send her ex a picture of it to boot. In reality, even if she had decided to move forward with the motion, the only people who really win in that kind of situation are the attorneys.

   Ultimately, however, I don't believe it's an attorney's role to make value judgments for their clients. If, after being told of the cost of moving forward to fight over the old couch, my client had still decided to do so for sentimental value, a sense of victory, or simply because she really liked burnt-orange velour— then more power to her. Who am I to tell someone their personal choice is wrong? My job as her attorney was to give her my professional advice, inform her about the cost of the process, and let her make the final, educated decision on how to move forward. If the attorney goes beyond that, it can get into pretty sticky territory.

While forgoing the couch made sense in this situation, that doesn't mean I advocate lying down and giving in to whatever the other party asks for just to get the process over as inexpensively as possible . What I do recommend is making decisions rationally and being prepared to pick your battles. The cold, hard truth is that neither party in a divorce is going to walk away with everything they wanted. While the old country song by Jerry Reed, "She Got the Gold Mine and I Got the Shaft," might scare you into thinking divorce is an all or nothing affair, in reality that's almost never the case.

Like I noted earlier, there are some circumstances when it's impossible for a divorcing couple to simply work things out amongst themselves, particularly when children are involved. If each parent truly believes that the children should live with them during the school week and the other parent every-other weekend, it can be hard to find a solution where one party doesn't get the proverbial gold mine and the other gets the shaft. In this case, having a good attorney can be very valuable. A knowledgeable third party can help identify creative solutions— such as a non-traditional schedule, use of a parenting consultant, or regular parenting reviews—that allow the parents to move forward without going through the expense and emotional toll of a full-blown trial. When it comes down to it though, everyone involved should really be thinking about what's best for the children, not what's best for the adults .

So, given all of this knowledge, what can you do to control costs in your own divorce? First and foremost, establish a line of communication with your ex, pony up for a few difficult discussions, and come to whatever agreements you can. There are certainly situations where this is not an option, such as if domestic violence has occurred or if one party has become verbally or emotionally abusive. However, it is worth making the effort for most couples. Anytime you're able to take an issue off the table by solving it without an attorney is time well-spent and dollars saved.

Next, do your best to keep an open mind and keep things moving. In all likelihood even if you're able to work some issues out there will still be a few points of disagreement between you and your ex. People usually get divorced because they couldn't see eye-to-eye during the marriage, so why should things be easier during the divorce, right? For the remaining issues, both emotional and monetary costs can be minimized if the parties take the alternative dispute process seriously—be it mediation, neutral evaluation, or something else.[1] Showing up to the session mentally prepared and ready to work out an agreement with the other party, no matter how hurt or angry you are, can only help in the long run.

Finally, make sure your expectations of what you hope to get out of the divorce are realistic. Discussing your goals for the case and whether they're in line with legal realities is one of the first things you should do with your attorney. Your attorney should have enough experience to know the strengths and weaknesses of your case and the likely outcomes of each contested issue. They should also have enough chutzpah to tell you when your expectations are a little out of whack. There's nothing more frustrating for my clients and me than when an opposing party is dead-set on a position that has little chance of succeeding in court, and their attorney hasn't advised them against it.

In a recent case, my client had a very strong claim to

---

1   Alternative Dispute Resolution (ADR) refers to any method that parties use to resolve a legal dispute outside of court. Except under rare circumstances, attempting to resolve a divorce outside of court is required before trial in Minnesota. Common forms of ADR in Minnesota are mediation, neutral evaluation, and binding arbitration.

spousal maintenance, which was validated both by a neutral evaluator and a temporary court order. The other party was dead-set against paying any spousal maintenance, took the case to trial, and couldn't have been clicking their heels over the result. I highly doubt that the other party's attorney sat him down for a reality check that could have saved the expense of trial and possibly achieved a better result through productive negotiations .

In the end, going through a divorce is an expensive and unpleasant experience no matter what. While I've had many clients manage to maintain a positive outlook throughout the process, and some who even threw "divorce parties" after it was all over, I'm sure every one of them could think of a million ways they would have rather spent their time and money. Divorce is never pretty, but there are ways to make it less painful. Taking the steps outlined above and making a commitment to yourself to get through the process as intelligently as possible will greatly influence how much time and money you spend on your attorney, and how much is left over to treat yourself to a vacation —or a new couch—afterward.

PART ONE
Chapter Two

Every Legal Brain has its Limits: Your attorney's knowledge is finite.

     As an attorney, I have a lot of attorney friends. Almost all of them are very smart individuals, but almost none of them (myself included) are as smart as they think they are. As the mustachioed whiz Albert Einstein famously said: "The difference between genius and stupidity is: genius has its limits." No matter how smart, experienced, or well-endowed with facial hair your family law attorney may be, their genius has its limits. The smartest ones are the ones that know that.

     Family law deals with an incredibly wide range of legal areas and it would be impossible to be an expert in all of them. Some of my recent cases involved everything from tax, real estate, and business entity issues, to matters of immigration, military jurisdiction, and health care. Even if I spent every waking hour studying, I still wouldn't be able to keep up with the latest developments in every aspect of law that affects the lives of my clients.

     As a born "do-it-yourselfer," this is a hard pill to swallow. My natural instinct is to jump in and learn as I go, but that's obviously not always the wisest decision. The last time I was working on one of my old cars I decided it needed a fresh coat of paint. I went ahead and attempted it myself, even though I'd never tried before. Car paint Picasso, I am not. It didn't turn out well, and I realized pretty quickly that I should stick to rebuilding engines. Goofing up a paint job isn't a big deal in the grand scheme of things, but goofing up a divorce is another matter. After accidentally defacing my old Fiat I simply sanded off the paint and took it to someone who knew what they were doing. Unfortunately, you can't sand off an unfavorable custody arrangement or an unforeseen tax snafu after a poorly handled divorce. A botch like that costs a lot more than a can of paint does.

Most practicing divorce attorneys acquire a basic knowledge of tax law, real estate law, bankruptcy law, immigration law, and other areas they encounter in cases. However, the really smart and experienced divorce attorneys recognize their limitations and develop a network of true experts to call on for help when complex situations arise. I personally would be lost without my trusted tax attorney, financial planner, bankruptcy attorney, child psychologist, and mortgage broker. Those divorce attorneys that pretend to have it all covered are likely letting a big head get in the way of what's best for the client. Every Batman needs his Robin. As attorneys, we need about twelve.

Of course, tapping specialized experts is not free. As with anything during the divorce process, you and your attorney should perform a simple cost-benefit analysis to see if expert involvement is right for you. I've encountered cases in which there were little to no assets to divide and the assets that did exist were straightforward. However, one party's attorney insisted upon the use of a certified divorce financial planner—to the tune of about two thousand dollars. It was pure overkill and a waste of the client's money. Financial planners are often great tools in divorce cases, but sometimes so is a simple Excel spreadsheet.

Before choosing a divorce attorney, try to identify the potential complications involved with your situation. If you have a house that will need to be refinanced or sold under difficult circumstances, ask a prospective attorney what Realtor and mortgage officer they work with to assess its worth. If you have pension plans to divide, ask what actuary they use to determine present day values. If there are financial assets to divide, especially if spousal maintenance is at issue, ask what tax expert the attorney will be consulting. Unless you are confident that your case is very straightforward, be wary of attorneys who claim to be able to do everything on their own.

I'm a big fan of quality quotes, so in the spirit of spreading the wisdom I think it's only appropriate that I end this chapter the way I started it. In the words of another very smart person, Mr. Woodrow Wilson: "I not only use all the brains that I have, but all I can borrow."

PART ONE
Chapter Three

The Search: Google Esq. is not a reliable source of advice

I love the internet. More specifically, I love Googling. When I'm sitting at work wondering what to make for dinner, there's nothing better than typing a few words in the search box and, one chicken chili recipe later, voila! Problem solved. The internet is obviously super useful for a lot of things, but its very nature as a public forum can also create a lot of problems. I'm sure I could do a Google search for exact numbers, but I'm just going to bet that the amount of misinformation circulating on the internet is greater than or equal to the amount of fact. There's often no reliable way to verify the author's identity, intentions, or knowledge level, and despite this, too many consumers take everything on the internet at face value .

Of course, there are still plenty of trustworthy resources available on the internet and many of them are free to the public. But even generally respected sites like WebMD can create problems if used incorrectly. I can only imagine how many physicians have run-ins with patients that wrongly self-diagnose a condition and later refuse to accept their doctor's professional advice. These patients apparently prefer to believe that entering a few symptoms on a website is an accurate substitute for many years of medical school and work experience. Just as it doesn't work for medical knowledge, trust me: it doesn't work for the law either.

Let's do an experiment. Just for fun, Google the words "alimony laws Minnesota" and see what pops up. When I ran that search, most of the results were law firm websites and paid listings for attorneys. When I clicked on the top listing, "five things you should know about divorce alimony laws in Minnesota," I was taken to www.laws.com, which is actually a paid attorney referral service. The specific page I landed on was titled "alimony in Minnesota" and was full of enough baloney to make a sandwich, albeit not a very good one. For starters, the term "alimony" hasn't been used in Minnesota law for many years. The meat of the article contained many statements that are at best generalizations, and more accurately, complete falsehoods. Remember, this is the top search result, not the obviously questionable Yahoo! Answers forum thread you might find three pages deep.

It's easy to see how relying on this web page might get someone into trouble. For example, say we have a young couple who've only been married for a year when one party decides that he or she wants a divorce. Let's say the wife (we'll call her Trudy) is a house painter and earns thirty-five thousand dollars a year, and the husband (we'll call him Ricardo) is in his first year of a PhD program. Coming into the marriage, Trudy had a hundred thousand dollars in the bank from a lucky casino visit years ago, and Ricardo had eighty thousand dollars in student loan debt from his undergraduate degree and Master's program. Ricardo, curious about spousal maintenance in Minnesota, hits up ol' Google search and finds www.laws.com. Ricardo, of course, doesn't know that laws.com is a paid referral site and not much of an authority on actual law, despite its impressive sounding domain name. Applying the criteria laid out in the article on alimony in Minnesota to his situation, Ricardo believes he is clearly entitled to spousal maintenance, both as a property equalizer and because he's a full-time student. In reality, however, he's entitled to no such thing. [2]

In this example, there is no property equalization necessary. Trudy's bank account balance and Ricardo's debt are

---

2   Without getting too detailed, property equalizers are generally used to make sure each party walks away from the marriage with a similar amount of marital assets and debts. Spousal maintenance is often awarded when one spouse has a financial need, and the other has extra income and can contribute to that need.

likely both non-marital. And even though Ricardo has three more years of school before he earns his PhD, he is able-bodied and has the current ability to work and earn his own living. Given the circumstances of the marriage—Trudy's modest income, Ricardo's present ability to work, the short duration of the marriage, the parties' youth, education levels and earning potentials—it's incredibly unlikely that any court would award spousal maintenance. I've seen this scenario countless times. The party relying on Google/what-happened-in-their-buddy's-divorce/what-a-paralegal-tells-them tends to dig in their heels on an untenable position, then is ultimately disappointed when they find out that what they thought they knew for sure was actually quite wrong.

A recent case of mine followed the above example almost to a tee. The parties had been married for about eight years, lived a modest life, and had earned approximately equal incomes during the marriage. The husband had recently quit his job to start an online business, which didn't go over so well with his wife, who I was representing. The husband had also acquired a new significant other, which, you guessed it, also didn't go over so well with my client. The husband and wife decided to divorce. After consulting the internet, the husband was convinced that he was entitled to spousal maintenance. He even forwarded an email from a friend of his who went to law school in Minnesota (but had apparently never handled a divorce case in his life) confirming his claim to spousal maintenance. I told my client that it was very unlikely spousal maintenance would be awarded in this case for a variety of reasons. Not surprisingly it wasn't, but a lot of extra time and money were spent going through a neutral evaluation on something that would have been a non-issue had the husband obtained competent legal advice in the first place.

Am I telling you to shut off your computer and never trust anything you find on the internet again? Heck no. After I head home from work tonight I'll be enjoying a glass of delicious homemade cinnamon-apple wine, crafted with equipment I purchased online and a recipe I found on a winemaking forum. Overall, the internet has been a good friend to both me and my stomach, and I would never say otherwise. What I would say, though, is that everything has its limitations and the internet is chief among them. Sure, it's great for looking up song lyrics or the latest cat meme, but legal advice? Eh, not so much. Being an attorney is a lot more complicated than looking up some supreme court rulings on Google or memorizing a few statutes. If it wasn't, well, let's just say there are a lot of masochistic law school students out there.

Especially in family law, the nuances of each client's situation—which can include external factors like the judge assigned to the case and case law that changes almost weekly—make it impossible to apply blanket statements or general legal advice in good faith. Each client I've worked with truly is unique, and while parts of someone's life might be similar to other clients I've had, no two situations are ever exactly the same. The anonymity and generality of the internet make it a pretty poor substitute for a real attorney who will take the time to get to know you and your unique situation. Use the internet for finding recipes, sharing pictures, and buying a rare coin collection on eBay; leave the legal advice to the professionals. You, and your wallet, will be glad you did.

PART ONE
Chapter Four

A Penny Saved Isn't Always a Penny Earned: You probably don't need the most expensive attorney you can find, but you probably shouldn't hire the cheapest either

Most reputable family law attorneys charge by the hour. Just in Minneapolis, I've seen attorneys charge anywhere from one hundred and forty to three hundred and eighty dollars for an hour of their time. Generally speaking, well-established attorneys who practice in the big downtown firms tend to be on the higher end of the spectrum, and newer attorneys who are on their own tend to be on the cheaper end.

Looking at the two objectively, you'd assume that going with the one hundred and forty an hour attorney would save some considerable dough, right? But looking a little closer you'll find that's not necessarily the case. Likewise, picking the more expensive option may not be as big a rip-off as it seems. Because the less expensive attorney is likely less experienced than the downtown attorney, he'll probably need to do more research to prepare for your case. Research takes time, and as we all know time is money—your money. It's also possible that the less expensive attorney is less skilled, which could lead to you losing out in the long run. The more expensive attorney is more expensive for a reason, but unless you have a case that has very complex issues, hiring the most expensive attorney available is probably overkill.

Besides the experience and the fancy office, do clients really get more by hiring a high-priced attorney? In typical lawyer fashion, the most accurate answer I can provide is yes and no. The big firm attorneys do have certain support and benefits that solo practitioners can't match. Big firms have dedicated researchers and law librarians to assist their attorneys. Big firms have the most up-to-date computer programs and access to certain financial planning tools that many solo practitioners do not. Big firms have posh conference rooms and fancy coffee drinks to make you feel pampered during your visit. Of course, the overhead cost of maintaining all of this is extremely high and is passed on to you in the form of higher hourly rates.

The least expensive attorneys often work from home or a virtual office (which usually includes a special mailing address and a rent-by-the-hour conference room). They most likely do not have support staff, or access to Westlaw or other expensive legal research software. Many specialize in uncontested divorces and have little to no experience dealing with disagreements that might arise later on.[3] Very few have any experience working for an established firm and may be extremely new to the profession. This is not to say that it's impossible to find a good attorney at a cheap price though. Some of the best legal minds I know have only been practicing a few years, and there's certainly nothing wrong with saving on overhead by working from a home office.

While most small or solo firms don't offer the same amenities as the big guys, they're not without their own advantages. If you decide to go with a smaller practice you'll probably get to work directly with an attorney as opposed to an assistant or paralegal. I've witnessed many clients meet their big-firm attorney for the first time when they show up to the courthouse on the day of the proceedings. That's an extremely unlikely scenario in a smaller firm. Further, I can honestly that say as the owner of a small firm I actually much prefer my office environment to the typical big firm downtown. My firm is in a modern loft-style office located in a historic building that's also home to many artist studios and small business owners. We don't have marble countertops or sixty-second floor views like

3   "Uncontested" divorces refer to the fairly common situation in which both parties are in complete agreement on all issues, and no negotiations or court appearances are necessary, only the drafting and signing of a divorce decree.

the big guys, but our space is sleek, inviting, and completely unique. Like many other small firms, I enjoy creating an atmosphere that's comfortable for my clients but has a little more character than, say, Mr. Duckworth's downtown digs.

As with most things in life, there are actually many shades of gray between the hyper-expensive attorney and his bargain-basement counterpart. Most people not named Denny Hecker would be best off choosing an attorney that is somewhere in between Fendi and Jordache. For some people, the expensive Fendi purse is worth it to them, and for some people the cheap Jordache purse will do just fine. In my very limited understanding of purse brands, it seems that most people want something closer to a Coach: well-made, has plenty of pockets (or whatever it is that one looks for in a purse), and can be purchased for less than the GDP of a small country. Okay, so I should probably stick to car analogies from here on out, but you get the picture.

Whatever kind of attorney you end up choosing, expect to put down a chunk of money as a retainer to get the process started. Make sure to read and sign a retainer contract that defines the terms of the fee agreement between you and your attorney. The initial chunk will be deposited into a separate account controlled by your attorney and transferred into their regular bank account as it is billed against. For example, if your attorney bills you five hundred dollars in a given month, they'll deduct five hundred dollars from your five thousand dollar retainer account and transfer it to their own account. In the retainer agreement it's important to make sure that any amount you put down is refundable. In the event that you decide to switch attorneys or not go forward with the legal action, you should be entitled to whatever funds are remaining in your retainer account without hassle.

There's one other type of attorney that we haven't talked about yet, and that's the attorney who's willing to work on a flat-fee basis instead of charging by the hour. In my professional opinion flat-fee attorneys should be avoided. Family law cases vary tremendously in the number of billable hours they take to complete and it's nearly impossible for a client to come out ahead in a flat fee arrangement. Once the attorney gets paid for their work up front, it's always in their best interest to resolve the case with as little work and time as possible. Cases that have issues that require research, negotiation, or dispute resolution most likely won't get the attention they deserve from a flat-fee attorney. And simple cases that don't require much effort on the attorney's part would cost less if the attorney was paid by the hour instead.

Worst of all, flat-fees are generally non-refundable, so once you pay your attorney a flat fee you are essentially locked in. If they don't return your phone calls, tough cookies. If they pressure you to settle when you know the offer isn't right for you, too bad. The advertisement on the bus stop bench for the eight hundred and ninety-nine dollar flat-fee divorce may be tempting, but trust me, you'll regret it. After the inevitable expenses, upgrades, and fee charges are tacked on, the actual price ends up being well over what was advertised anyway.

Overall, the best advice I can give you is to choose an attorney based on the specific needs of your case. If you're going through an ugly divorce with multi-million dollar hidden assets, complex business ownership disputes, and pending deportation issues, you might want the best attorney money can buy. If you only need an attorney to draft a simple uncontested modification of child support, the inexpensive route is the probably the better way to go. For the majority of people going through a divorce, an attorney in the middle price range who can give you effective representation without charging and arm and a leg is almost always the best option.

PART ONE
Chapter Five

Character 101: Your attorney's personality WILL have an impact on your case

Believe it or not, attorneys are human beings. Just like doctors, mechanics, sanitation workers, and everyone else on the planet who is not comatose, lawyers have individual personalities that influence how we conduct our daily business. I've gotten to know the local family law community pretty well in my four years of practice in Minneapolis (plus my time practicing in small-town Minnesota before that), and I can confidently say that there's no such thing as a "typical" family law attorney. Some are soft-spoken, some are ultra-aggressive, some are serious, some are jovial, some are cocky, some are friendly, and some are difficult. There are attorneys that I like and some that I'm not a huge fan of, and despite my rakish good looks, I'm sure there are other attorneys that feel the same way about me.

Unlike your preferred mechanic or local letter carrier, your attorney's personality has a huge impact on the outcome of their work. Regardless of whether your mechanic is the most cantankerous or friendliest person in town, your alternator will be replaced the same way. However, if your attorney has, for example, a very aggressive personality, issues in a divorce that may otherwise be amicably negotiated between the parties may instead wind their way through the adversarial process and end up in the courtroom. Conversely, a divorce attorney who is conflict-averse—and yes, they do exist—may push the same client toward settlement on terms that aren't particularly favorable, just to avoid the risk of going to trial.

I've encountered several attorneys in my own practice whose personalities have greatly influenced the course of a case. A few years ago I handled a case in which the opposing counsel had a very empathetic, emotional personality and really took her client's story to heart. Empathy like this can certainly be a positive thing, but it can also cause an attorney to partially lose the ability to objectively reason—one of the most essential parts of practicing law.

In this case, I represented a father who petitioned to establish custody. The mother had firmly dug in her heels on the position that their child should have no contact with my client whatsoever, due to his past chemical abuse issues and her dislike for his current significant other. Any experienced custody attorney knows that the burden for eliminating parental contact is incredibly high in Minnesota and wasn't going to being met under these circumstances. However, because Mom's attorney was so emotionally involved in her client's situation, she was unable to give her client an objective, professional opinion and dug her heels in just as hard as Mom did. The case ended up in the courtroom, and my client was awarded far more parenting time with fewer restrictions than what he had asked for during negotiations. Mom's attorney was not a bad attorney overall, but her personality was not particularly well-suited for this case and ended up having a negative impact on the outcome.

Another common personality type that I encounter in my work is the old-school, bulldog attorney. Now I don't use the terms "bulldog" and "old-school" as insults, though they sometimes carry that connotation outside of law. The family court system has shifted in recent years to require mediation, neutral evaluation, and other forms of alternative dispute resolution in custody or divorce cases in order to avoid time in the court room. Prior to these requirements, attorneys would traditionally exchange mountains of discovery requests, engage in costly custody studies, hire financial experts to determine values of assets, and build a case against the other party.[4]

---

4   We'll go over discovery methods and expert evaluations in much more
    detail in part two, but for now it'll suffice to say that they are all expensive

Nowadays, before any of this expensive process begins parties typically engage in early neutral evaluation to see if a settlement can be reached first. The success rate with these new processes is around ninety-percent—not too shabby. In my experience, old-school attorneys may have a harder time taking off their adversarial hat and coming to the table to try and work things out together. Again, this doesn't mean they are ineffective attorneys or litigators, it just means their style is not well-suited for some cases.

For example, I recently handled a case in which the parties had no children or major assets. We engaged in the early neutral evaluation process and the parties were poised to reach an agreement consistent with the neutral evaluator's recommendation. After working diligently for over four hours in the session, opposing counsel abruptly stopped the process and announced that he couldn't allow his client to reach an agreement until formal discovery had been completed. I reminded him that the whole point of the neutral evaluation process was to avoid the expense of things like discovery, but he insisted on proceeding in an old-school fashion. We exchanged discovery requests, sent documents back and forth, swapped offer letters and phone calls, and eventually settled on the exact terms recommended by the evaluator. The only difference was that the final divorce decree was delayed by almost five months and the legal bills for each party had increased by several thousand dollars, which neither of them had to spare.

I know what you're thinking: this is all nice information, Zach, but how exactly am I supposed to predict my attorney's personality and its possible impact on my case? Well, short of presenting potential attorneys with a Myers-Briggs personality test at initial consultation, there are a few things you can do. First, before you even begin attorney shopping, lay out the facts

---

and time-consuming methods of gathering information and preparing for trial.

of your case and try to imagine what personality style would be best suited to them. If spousal maintenance and property division are the main issues in your divorce and you suspect your ex is hiding a sizable chunk of change in an offshore bank account, you'll want a more aggressive, litigation-focused attorney. If you're mainly concerned about working together to smoothly transition your young children into a co-parenting situation, avoiding a staunch, bulldog attorney will likely make the process easier.

In reality most cases don't fall neatly into either end of the extreme spectrum, and finding an attorney with some balance of both bulldog and "Kumbaya" qualities is usually best. The attorneys I respect the most are incredibly gifted at working together and negotiating when it's time to negotiate, and skillfully arguing in court when it's time to advocate. Don't be afraid to ask potential attorneys about this straight up. See where they stand on the issue and if you're not comfortable with it or you don't feel it's a good fit for your case, then don't hire them. Yes, we are human, but we're not going to feel bad if you don't think we're the right fit. Always ask questions up front and be open about what you're looking for.

So, you've found an attorney whose professional style seems right for your case and you think you're ready to go. Your initial consultation was a little awkward and your phone conversations are somewhat off, but that's no big deal. Soon, however, you find yourself dreading going into the office. It seems like your personal communication styles just don't mesh that well, leading to uncomfortable meetings. But you're paying your attorney to provide you with a professional service, not to be your best friend, right? Well, not exactly. While your attorney's professional prowess is certainly more important than their taste in music, if you can't relate to them on a personal level you might find the process feels much more difficult than it needs to.

Going through a divorce or child custody case is stressful enough as it is, and phone conversations or office visits with your attorney shouldn't be a chore. Finding an attorney you can relate to will make communication more natural and will help develop a sense of trust and understanding between you both, which is invaluable in achieving a good end result. It doesn't hurt if they're a good conversationalist, make you feel at ease, or throw a few jokes out to lighten the mood as well. You're going to be spending a significant amount of time and money with this person, so it may as well be someone you like, right? As an added bonus, attorneys who are generally liked by their clients are often also liked by opposing counsel, court personnel, and the bench, which can never be a bad thing. I consider it the highest form of compliment when a former client says they'd like to grab a beer with me after the case is over—and it's even better when the opposing counsel does too!

Until a day comes when lawyers have their own trading cards listing important statistics and personality traits (I'd want to have the card closest to the chalky bubble gum, so mine would always smell the best in the pack), you'll have to do a little homework on your own. Meet your attorney in person, ask questions, get to know them as much as you can, and carefully consider if they're going to be a good fit both professionally and personally. If you take the time to do this at the start of the process, chances are you'll be much happier at the end.

PART ONE
Chapter Six

All by Myself: You may not even need an attorney

Let's revisit our old friend Google for a minute. Grab your computer, open an internet browser, and go to www.mncourts.gov. This is the Minnesota Judicial Branch website, and on it, you'll find a self-help section with a wealth of DIY forms for everything from suing your landlord to changing your name. Try clicking on the link for divorce, custody, and family law. You'll see that while there's no personalized information or legal advice available, there are a number of fairly comprehensive forms covering many common family law scenarios. Looking at this website it's pretty easy to see why many people might be tempted to tackle a divorce without help from an attorney, right?

For better or worse, but mostly because my career prospects as a professional athlete were dim, I chose to become an attorney. I'd like to think that a set of online forms hasn't made me obsolete, but I'm aware that some people see these DIY forms and think just that. If you're a person who believes that all a lawyer does is fill out some forms and mail them to a judge, then why would you pay them two hundred dollars an hour to do what you could do yourself for free? My own brother is in that camp, and he reminds me of it during bowling league whenever he gets a chance. As I tend to do with everything (if you hadn't noticed), I usually respond to him with an auto repair analogy, since that, at least, is something we can see eye-to-eye on.

When something is wrong with your car you can either bring it into the shop or consult a repair manual and attempt to fix it yourself. For someone with a strong DIY spirit and a basic understanding of automobiles, handling oil changes and coolant flushes is a good way to save a little dough. If you're feeling brave, have the right tools, and own an older car that's easier to work with, you may even decide to step it up a notch and replace a worn alternator. But if you need a major repair to your engine or transmission, only have a roll of duct tape and a screwdriver to your name, or you own a new car with a more complicated design, you're probably going to want to head on down to the shop. Breaking out the ratchet set and jack stands may seem like a good idea at the time, but chances are you'll inadvertently do more harm than good to your car and end up at the repair shop anyway. Except this time, you'll have to spend three month's salary paying the mechanic to undo the damage of your handiwork.

The same basic principle applies to family law. If you have a straightforward case and a strong desire to carry a briefcase, you can go it alone in the legal system. A simple modification of child support after your child turns eighteen is a good example of something that many people can handle without an attorney. Changing your child's name and setting up initial establishment of child support by yourself are some other reasonably safe bets, as long as there are no other complications or conflicts with your ex. [5]

Anything more complex than that is a whole different ball of wax. If you and your ex have only been married a year or two, you don't have kids, a house, or a retirement plan to deal with, and you agree on all matters pertaining to your separation, it is possible to go through a divorce without hiring an attorney to represent you. Even then I would strongly suggest having a lawyer draft the agreement with your ex, or, if nothing else, at least have them review the paperwork you plan to file. A divorce affects nearly every aspect of your life, and unless you're

---

5   Child support can present tricky situations however, especially if one party has varying income levels, is self-employed, or is suspected of hiding income or intentionally under-earning. In those situations, it is definitely worthwhile to have an attorney work with you.

completely confident that your case is simple and your ex is on the same page no matter what the variable, there's too much at stake to risk doing it wrong. If there are children, a home or business, or financial assets involved, don't even consider divorcing without an attorney. Just like trying to rebuild a modern, computer-controlled automatic transmission in your backyard, it's a situation just begging for disaster. I have yet to meet anyone who has attempted a child custody matter on their own and didn't live to regret it later. You wouldn't put the engine of your 2012 Accord at stake, so why would you risk putting your kids, your home, or your livelihood at stake?

Unfortunately, despite the risks, some people do still put these things in peril. One of the hardest, and sadly most common, scenarios that family law attorneys encounter in our practice are parents who established custody or went through a divorce by themselves and later come to us asking to undo what they had done. It's always incredibly difficult to tell someone that even if they had not fully understood what they agreed to initially, there's little hope that it can be fixed once it's been done. The system is set up to avoid giving anyone a second bite at the proverbial apple, so if something isn't done right the first time, it is often close to impossible to correct it later. It may be a little more expensive to do it right the first time, but the emotional and legal costs of an attempted redo far surpass that.

If you don't think you need to hire an attorney to walk you through each step but you don't want to risk doing everything on your own, there are viable alternatives to the traditional court process. If you and your ex are able to work together and come to a full agreement, hiring an attorney simply to draft and explain the documents can be an option. Not only will this save you money, it will also save you peace of mind when you walk away knowing there was a professional there to ask questions and identify any areas of the agreement you may have missed. If you and your ex are committed to working together to develop a custody agreement and parenting schedule, consider working directly with a qualified mediator or neutral evaluator instead of each of you hiring your own counsel. But if you have issues that you and your ex are not able to resolve on your own, all is not lost. The guidance and experience that a good mediator or evaluator brings to the table is often the push people need to come to an agreement while still avoiding the traditional court process.

Additionally, there are attorneys who practice collaborative law, which is designed to help couples work through issues and stay out of the court room.[6] My firm offers a unique process involving mediation, evaluation, and arbitration that guarantees a resolution without setting foot in court, even if the parties get stuck on certain issues. The one option I would strongly caution against is the use of a paralegal to help resolve your issue. Paralegals, while often incredibly talented and smart, have never argued inside a courtroom, are not licensed to practice law, and aren't qualified to draft legal agreements for clients or licensed to give out legal advice. You wouldn't take cooking advice from someone's who's never been in the kitchen, right?

Just as you don't need to take your car to the shop after every little bump in the road, you don't need to run to a lawyer either. Hiring an attorney is often necessary in family law matters, but that doesn't mean you'll be spending your savings in the courtroom. A good attorney will not only use their creativity and negotiation skills to help you avoid the courtroom now, they'll also help you avoid it in the future by reaching a solid conclusion the first time. When you hire a quality mechanic to repair your car problem, you know you won't be coming back any

---

6   Collaborative attorneys do not go to court – an agreement is signed at the outset of representation stating that neither attorney will represent their client in court, but instead will work to resolve the case through negotiation and ADR. If the case is unable to resolve, the parties must hire different attorneys to work through the court process.

time soon. The same rule applies with attorneys, and we won't get grease on your hand saying goodbye, either.

PART ONE
Chapter Seven

Finding the One: Do your research before signing on the dotted line

All attorneys licensed in Minnesota are *authorized* to handle your divorce or custody case; however, not all attorneys licensed in Minnesota are *qualified* to handle it. Technically speaking, I could defend one client against a murder charge, set up a complex trust for a second client, and handle the details of a merger for my third client's business. But they would most likely end up in jail, broke, and working at McDonald's, and I would have a pretty bum ego to massage. Even though I'm licensed to practice in business law, criminal law, and many other areas, I only practice in family law because that's what I know, and that's what I am good at.

Most attorneys in today's market have evolved from generalists to specialists, especially those that practice in bigger cities where there's more competition. I began my career in small-town Minnesota working at a general practice law firm, and let me tell you, it was not for me. At one point I was handling a major conflict with a health insurance company, a contract claim, a small business shareholder dispute, several criminal cases, and an array of family law cases simultaneously. With the exception of bankruptcy and patents cases, if it came in the door we'd figure out a way to handle it. It isn't easy shifting gears from business law to probate to property law, and I have a lot of respect for general practitioners who do on a daily basis. However, my experience tells me that most clients are better served by going to someone who handles a more narrow range of topics. It's hard enough keeping up on all of the trends and developments in family law; I can't imagine adding any more to my plate.

Many firms narrow their focus even further and become experts in a very specialized area of law. I have friends who are family law attorneys but focus their practice on international divorce, grandparent visitation, or LGBT issues. For someone with a very unique set of circumstances, having an attorney that specializes in cases like theirs can be extremely beneficial.

The vast majority of people with a common family law matter like divorce, custody, or adoption just want to know where to find a good attorney. There's certainly no shortage of options in Minnesota and the choices can seem overwhelming at first. Try Googling "Minneapolis divorce lawyers" and see how many pages come up. I stopped counting on page fifty-two.

Faced with that daunting list of names, what can you do to start narrowing the field? First, make sure the attorney you're checking out has handled your kind of case recently. If you're going through a divorce and you find a family law practice that only advertises adoption services, you can obviously strike that one off the list. But don't rely on websites and Google's top results only. A firm's website is used as a marketing tool and will often say whatever it takes to get you in the door. And those firms that show up in the top results have usually paid Google or manipulated their advertising to get there.

If you find an attorney that looks promising but want to know more, a really helpful trick is to do a case search on the Minnesota Judicial Branch website (www.mncourts.gov). Click on "find a court case," then "access trial case records." Click "I accept,", then "Civil, Family & Probate Case Records". In the drop-down box, select "search by Attorney", then input the attorney's name, the annoying anti-spam security letters, and click search. For example, type in my name, Zachary Smith, on an attorney search and you'll get several pages of results. Most of them will say "dissolution" (divorce), "custody," or "expedited process" (child support) under the case type column. If you run this search on an attorney you're interested in and you get very few results or the ones you do are very different from your kind of case, be wary that the attorney may not have much experience.

It's also a good idea to run a discipline check on any attorney you're considering before signing the retainer agreement. The bar association makes discipline records publicly available on the internet. Any attorney who is not currently licensed to practice law or has a spotty ethical record should obviously be avoided. Be cautious of any endorsement services too. Designations like "super lawyer" and ratings on sites like Avvo.com are often related more to an attorney's advertising budget than their professional skill.

As with most services, the best way to find a good attorney is often through referral. If you've tapped your personal and professional network and come up with nothing, try reaching out to a realtor, financial planner, or family therapist. Believe it or not, they almost always know a good attorney and will be more than happy to refer you. Other attorneys are also a great referral source if they don't practice the type of law you're looking for. Remember in Chapter Two when I said every good attorney has a network of experts in their rolodex? Attorneys tend to get a lot of questions from family and friends that fall way outside our areas of expertise, and I'm always glad to give out the number for my friend the tax attorney, criminal defense lawyer, or bankruptcy pro to help them out. Likewise, the vast majority of my business comes from referrals from other attorneys or professionals who trust me to take care of any clients they send my way.

Ultimately, the most important part of your attorney search is the initial consultation. Meet with your prospective attorney in-person and get to know a little about them. Though we fantasized about lawyer trading cards in Chapter Five, there's really no substitution for the gut-feeling test. If you feel comfortable with your prospective attorney and the attorney sounds like he or she knows what they're talking about, then go for it. If your communication styles clash, they sound a bit unsure of themselves, and you walk out feeling not like it's not quite the right fit, then it probably isn't. If your initial meeting is troublesome, it probably won't be any better later when you start dealing with opposing counsel or hit the courtroom.

While you probably don't want a pushy salesman type who will tell you whatever you want to hear to get you to sign the retainer agreement; you do need someone who understands the law, can communicate effectively, and inspires confidence in their abilities. If you don't get a good feeling from the initial consultation, try another attorney on for size and see how it goes. Consultations are almost always free, so don't be afraid to shop around. Hiring an attorney is an important choice that can have a serious impact on your life. Take the time to do your research and get it right before signing on the proverbial dotted line—you'll be glad you did.

PART TWO
Chapter One

Revving the Engine of Justice: Petition, answer, and ICMC

Let's say you've got a legal action you want to take care of, but you're not sure how to get the ball rolling. You could put on a nice outfit and roam the streets in hopes that you cross paths with a magical judge who solves all your problems, but that's probably not the most efficient (or sane) way to go. When someone wants to initiate an action in family court regarding divorce or child custody in Minnesota, they begin the process by serving a petition and summons on the opposing party and filing it with the county court.[7] The initial petition contains basic identifying information about the parties, lists out the issues at stake, and describes what the petitioning person is asking the court to do (e.g., grant a divorce, award custody of children, etc.). The petition is served on your ex along with a summons, which contains some conditions each party must follow. This will include a prohibition on canceling your spouse's insurance coverage or making large, unnecessary expenditures while a divorce is pending. The summons also informs the other party that they must provide a formal answer to the petition within a specified time period, which is usually thirty days.

I've encountered a lot of people who get confused about what a formal answer actually entails. Just yesterday I received a phone call from someone who had been served with a petition several months ago. I asked him if he had filed an answer yet, and he was under the impression that the phone call he made to his wife's attorney sufficed as an answer. I let him know that probably didn't count, and a formal answer and counter-petition

---

7   "Serving" in this case means having a third-party, such as a process server or the sheriff hand the documents to the other party. Filing involves sending those same documents to the county court, along with a filing fee to get the court process started.

needed to be served and filed ASAP to avoid the very real possibility of his wife proceeding by default without him. The formal answer is the served party's opportunity to let the court know if they disagree with any parts of the petition. Sometimes none of the identifying facts are in dispute and can simply be admitted. However, if an opposing party wants to have any say in the potential end-result, they should answer the petition and include a counter-petition identifying his or her own desired end-result, as it differs from their ex's.

Petitions are pretty straightforward documents. When filing a petition it is important to list everything that is being requested of the court, but it is not necessary to get super specific this early in the proceedings. For example, if the parties have bank accounts to divide up, the petition may ask for the court to "fairly and equitably divide the bank accounts." That lets the court know what's being requested without getting muddled too deep in details that will be established later down the line. Although brevity is the name of the petition game, it's important to not miss any issues on the table. For example, if the initial petition does not have a request for spousal maintenance, no answer is provided, and the case moves forward by default. The court may not have the authority to order spousal maintenance. Since it was not asked for in the initial petition, the opposing party does not officially know the issue is even at stake. You can't give your coworker the stink-eye for eating the last piece of cake if you didn't tell him you were off your diet and needed a three o'clock sugar fix.

Take a look at an online sample divorce petition. It should be short, sweet, and to the point. It identifies all the parties and issues involved, but doesn't get into the nitty-gritty details. Petitions for other kinds of family law cases, like child custody, are similar in form and function. The petition has a place for the party's notarized signature and the party's attorney's signature, which verifies that the petition is brought for a valid reason and is truthful to the best of everyone's knowledge.

Once the petitions, answers, and counter-petitions have all been filed (along with the accompanying document cocktail of the summons, certificate of representation, confidential information form, financial affidavit for child support, and sealed financial source document—shaken, not stirred) court administration will issue a date for the first hearing. In most metro counties the first hearing is called the initial case management conference (ICMC). Even though the ICMC takes place in a courtroom in front of a judge—complete with intimidating robe and gavel—I promise it's nothing to stress over. Anyone who has ever been through a divorce or custody battle can tell you that the ICMC is one of the easiest parts of the entire process.

While each Minnesota county does things slightly differently, the purpose of the hearing is largely the same: to give the court an idea of what issues are at stake, to decide on a method for attempting to resolve the case short of trial, and to give the parties an opportunity to meet the judge assigned to their case. Many counties hold this hearing off the record, meaning that no court reporter is present to record what is being said. Some judges won't wear the traditional robe and a few might even come and sit at a table with the parties.

After meeting everyone, the parties will usually agree upon a method of alternative dispute resolution (such as mediation or early neutral evaluation) and select the mediator or evaluator. If the parties have any agreements to present to the court, most judges will allow them to put the terms of the agreement on the record. For example, if everyone agrees on how much child support will be paid, the parties may put that agreement on the record right then and there to narrow the issues in dispute. However, judges will cut short any attempts either party makes to argue a disputed item at this point.

Even though the ICMC is a low-stress hearing, it's still

important to get it right. Specific paperwork must be filed prior to the hearing or a party may be sanctioned.[8] Also, any agreements that are put in to the record are binding, so you need to know exactly what you're agreeing to and the consequences of that agreement. It's critical to understand the differences between the alternative dispute resolution methods and to have an attorney who is familiar with the different mediators or evaluators. While all mediators and evaluators on a county's roster are required to meet certain standards, only your attorney will know one may be better suited to your case than others. Your attorney should go over the details of the process with you beforehand and make you as comfortable as possible. Attending an ICMC is never a day at the beach, but it shouldn't feel like a scene from *Jaws* either.

---

8   Each county has its own ICMC Data Sheet that is required to be completed and turned in before the hearing. Why there isn't a uniform format for the entire state is beyond me, but that is an issue for another day. Judges to tend to get upset, however, when parties use a different county's data sheet, or forget to file it altogether. As a rule, it's best to stay on the good side of your judge.

PART TWO
Chapter Two

Back it Up: Alternative Dispute Resolution

With over twenty thousand divorces and thousands of child custody matters filed each year, post-decree actions, and other legal disputes piled on top of that, it's easy to see why the Minnesota court system is routinely clogged up. If all of those cases went to trial, there would not be a plumber in the world that could save our ship. Even if only ten percent of family law cases went to trial, the system would be so overwhelmed it would take years, not months, to resolve a common divorce or custody matter in Minnesota.

Luckily, we've got an excellent plumber in the form of alternative dispute resolution. Reducing the stress on the court system is only one of the reasons alternative dispute resolution has become so prevalent in our state. As any judge or veteran attorney will tell you, the results achieved from the alternative dispute resolution process are almost always preferable to what is concocted by a judge after a contentious trial. The people most intimately involved in the case, the parties themselves, can almost always craft the best agreement. With limited understanding of the situation and only a few days, or possibly only a few hours, of "he-said, she-said" testimony to base a life-altering decision on, it is hard to expect much better out of a judge. This is exactly why alternative dispute resolution is such a powerful and effective tool. In my years of handling divorces and custody matters I've been consistently amazed by the number of people who've managed to push through extreme differences and find a workable compromise. With the help of a skilled mediator or neutral evaluator some of my toughest cases have reached a resolution, even when it seemed that a resolution was not possible.

The most common form of alternative dispute resolution practiced here is early neutral evaluation (ENE). To keep beating the plumbing metaphor to death, ENE is sort of like the plunger in alternative dispute resolution's tool belt. ENE is similar to traditional mediation, but has one very substantial twist. In mediation, the mediator is a facilitative neutral. This means that they may help the parties work through issues in the case and reach compromises, but the mediator cannot interject with their own opinion. The mediator is there to help facilitate discussion, keep the parties focused on the issues at hand, and maintain a productive conversation. Conversely, an experienced evaluator takes the place of the mediator in ENE. After a basic exchange of information, the evaluator provides an expert opinion of what may be a fair or likely outcome in the case. The neutral evaluator in effect simulates a judge at an informal, mini-trial setting. Unlike a judge, though, their final opinion is non-binding unless both parties agree to it, which often happens. Minus the snarky comments and TV drama, ENE is about as close as it gets to Judge Judy in the divorce or custody process.

There are two types of ENE in Minnesota: social and financial. Social ENE (SENE) deals with issues regarding child custody and parenting time. SENE sessions usually take place with a team of two evaluators, one male and one female.[9] Often times, one evaluator is an attorney and the other is an expert in the field of child development. The evaluators spend a great deal of time listening to each party describe their relationship with the children, their desired custody arrangement and schedule, and any concerns they may have with the other parent. The evaluators then come together and propose the custody and parenting time plan they feel is workable and in the best interests of the children, as well as in-line with what they believe

---

9   The SENE is generally handled by a male-female team so that neither parent feels that any gender bias affects the recommendation of the evaluators.

a judge would order if the case went to trial.

The Financial ENE (FENE), predictably, addresses financial issues such as division of property and financial accounts, spousal maintenance, retirement, and child support. Unlike the SENE, there is usually one evaluator involved, and the evaluator is usually an attorney or financial expert. The process for the FENE is similar to the SENE. Once an order is issued to participate in ENE and the evaluator is chosen, the parties submit certain relevant documents in preparation for the ENE session. The session typically lasts around four hours. At the FENE, the evaluator will listen to each party's side of the story and ask direct questions to clarify any gray areas. After gathering the necessary information, the evaluator will put together a proposed balance sheet and share their opinion as to what would be ordered in terms of spousal maintenance and child support if the case went to trial.

It might seem like attorneys ride the bench in an ENE game, but our role in the process is actually quite crucial. Unlike in litigation, the parties will do most of the talking at the ENE session. However, having representation throughout the ENE process is critical for many reasons. An experienced divorce and custody attorney will assess your situation and provide realistic expectations for a reasonable settlement before the ENE session begins. They will identify rights to property or custody issues that you likely would have missed on your own, work to select a qualified and favorable neutral for your case, and suggest creative solutions for problematic issues. Your attorney will advocate for you and help advance your position on any contested matters. Your attorney will eliminate the possibility of being bullied by an aggressive opposing counsel who may try to force an unfavorable settlement. Your attorney will also help prepare you for the process, and it's certainly a lot less stressful going through an unfamiliar procedure with someone by your side who's been there many, many times before.

Have I convinced you that attorneys are valuable members of the ENE team, yet? Okay, one more thought for good measure: Your attorney will draft the final divorce decree and make sure that any agreements reached are accurately reflected in the filings with the court, which is extremely important. Attorneys shoot, attorneys score! (But you get to keep the trophy.)

PART TWO
Chapter Three

Temporary Motions: Expensive, unpredictable, but sometimes necessary

Okay, so you've filed the petition, attended the ICMC, and gone through mediation or early neutral evaluation. You're already a few months into the divorce process and for some reason, there just seems to be no light at the end of the tunnel. You're about to begin preparing for a trial that is months, if not years, away. What happens if there are pressing issues to take care of in the meantime? What if you're unable to survive without spousal maintenance or child support from your ex? What if the two of you can't decide on a schedule for the kids? And who gets to live in the house while this whole mess is sorted out? These questions will get permanent answers eventually, but often "eventually" isn't good enough. This is when you might find yourself considering a motion for temporary relief.

Minnesota divorce law specifically allows parties to a divorce to bring a temporary motion to speed the resolution of issues like parenting time, custody, child support, spousal maintenance, payment of attorney fees, use of the home, and possession of personal property.[10] The decision reached in temporary proceedings cannot have any effect on the final outcome of contested issues, but the terms of the temporary order are in effect until the final divorce decree is issued, at which point the terms of final order rule. Think of it like a Band-Aid for a bullet wound. Temporary motions can momentarily stop the bleeding, but you're still going to need to get stitches eventually.

Here's an example where a temporary motion might be filed: Say a wife happens to earn a hundred thousand dollars a

_____
10   Mn. Stat. §518.131

year while the husband stays home with the three kids. He's going to need some cash from the wife to get by each month until the divorce is final. A lot of times, without receiving a temporary financial award, the lower-earning spouse is at a serious disadvantage during the divorce process. The spouse that earns more money can afford to drag out the litigation and knows the precarious position of their ex. Often times, the high-earner can use this position as leverage to pressure the other party into accepting a settlement offer that is unfavorable and they wouldn't otherwise accept. If money's tight and every day the divorce drags on is another precious dollar out of your pocket, chances are you're just going to want to get the whole thing over with as soon as possible. Filing a temporary motion can help ease the pressure and level the playing field, so that you're able to continue pursuing the most favorable final decree possible.

 With our imperfect system, naturally there are some serious pitfalls to consider before firing off a temp motion. Because the motion often takes place prior to discovery exchange and before much of the trial preparation and fact gathering has occurred, the parties are often working without knowing exactly what's on the table. Like trying to cook a meal without knowing what's in the fridge, the product can sometimes leave a bad taste. For example if one party owns a business, it's unlikely that a full valuation of the business worth has taken place or an accurate income level determined. It's tough to know how much money a party can afford to support their spouse if you don't know exactly what they've got to give in the first place. Any necessary custody evaluation has not yet taken place either, so parties are left to rely at least partially on using conjecture, inferences, and he-said-she-said evidence to prove that temporary relief should be granted.

 Judges are often put in the position of making their decision based on snap-judgments or an educated guess. It can be frustrating to ask a judge to order child support or spousal maintenance based your client's claim that "I know my husband does a ton of side work for cash and makes at least eighty thousand dollars a year," when you don't yet have the proof to back it up. That's not to say that I've never been successful with such arguments, but it's definitely not the ideal way to persuade the court of your viewpoint.

Temporary motions are often filed because someone doesn't have enough money to get by until the divorce, so a motion should ease your financial troubles, right? Not exactly. Unfortunately even if you're facing economic hardship, bringing a temporary motion is going to cost you, and it's not a quick fix either. Between drafting the necessary motion paperwork and affidavits, collecting information, scheduling a court date, preparing for the hearing, and attending the hearing, there's a lot of work involved.

It's safe to say that you won't make it through many temporary motions for less than a few thousand dollars in attorney's fees, and that's just the start of it. It will also take several months, at the earliest, to get from filing a motion to receiving an enforceable order. Except under the most extreme circumstances or when it's clear the divorce will drag on for a long time, it's my experience that focusing on working towards a final resolution is smarter than spending time and money pursuing a temporary order.

Sadly, the temporary proceeding is also the first instance in many divorces where people "go ugly." The affidavits submitted to support each party's position will usually contain allegations that are not particularly favorable to their ex. In the face of affidavits and arguments in open court, any spirit of cooperation that existed to that point usually finds a way of evaporating. While temporary orders can sometimes aid in reaching a fair settlement by leveling the playing field, I have yet to see a case where the parties get along better as a result of a temporary order.

      Temporary motion practice is a useful and necessary tool in certain situations, but I hope I convinced you by now that it should be used sparingly. If your case has gotten to the point where a temporary motion for relief is necessary, don't even think about trying to proceed without an experienced family law attorney. There's no form to fill out to initiate the process, but there will be a hearing in front of a judge, and the rules of evidence are enforced. You only get one shot at a good outcome, so make sure your ducks are in a row and don't blow it with bad aim.

PART TWO
Chapter Four

Discovery: Time to show your hand

Unlike in courtroom dramas you see on TV, there are no surprise witnesses or "gotcha!" documents produced by a crafty attorney in real trials. As much as I'd love to channel my inner Matlock and shock the audience with a perfectly timed bombshell in one of my cases, unfortunately I'll just have to keep living vicariously through reruns. In real life, each party knows exactly what's up the other side's sleeve. They know exactly who's going to testify and have seen all of the evidence and exhibits well before they are brought to the witness stand. In the next phase of the divorce process, called discovery, sharing is the name of the game.

In Minnesota family court, parties usually engage in what is known as informal discovery. In a nutshell, this means that each side simply tells the other side what documents they want, and everyone cooperates by providing what's requested. This might be financial statements, anything related to the house or vehicles, or work and income information. Things can get a little more intense when complicated issues like business ownership and valuation, health problems, and hidden off-shore bank accounts are involved. If either party isn't playing nice with the simple exchange of information or there are any complexities, that's when an attorney turns to their bag of tricks to get what's needed.

If you're curious and really want to do your homework, part five of the Minnesota Rules of Civil Procedure describes the discovery process and provides a checklist of available tools to gather information for trial.[11] In Minnesota, discovery is very

---

11   The Rules of Civil Procedure can be found on the Minnesota Judicial
     Branch website, http://www.mncourts.gov

liberal. The rules allow parties to request information or documents related to anything deemed relevant to a claim by either party, even if the particular evidence sought may not necessarily be admissible at trial. Except for a few limitations, the parties have a pretty free license to gather whatever they think might be useful to their case.

The first and most basic method for obtaining information is the request for production of documents. This is just what it sounds like: one party formally asks the other to produce a bunch of specific documents, and the other party must produce them within a specified time, generally thirty days. It's a useful tool for gathering things like bank statements, business accounting records, pay records, and so on. Of course, as nice as it would be if everyone followed the golden rule of Kindergarten, parties don't always play fair and produce everything they've been asked for. Making a document request is a simple and relatively inexpensive way to get the party started, like Pin the Tail on the Donkey or a bottle of fine malt liquor.

Employing written interrogation is another common technique for gathering information. Interrogatories are questions submitted to the other party that must be answered within thirty days. The questions can be about pretty much any topic relevant to the case, though occasionally you'll see questions that are clearly out of bounds. I remember a case in which the opposing party, who was unrepresented, sent thirty-six pages of interrogatories to his soon-to-be-ex-wife. Most of the questions were obviously intended to get under her skin. Some of the more colorful ones included: "Describe your experience as a prostitute," and "Tell me about the trip you just took to Mexico with your new boyfriend." Though this man was clearly more concerned with being immature than making a good case for himself, some more useful questions may have been: "Describe the benefits available through your current employer," or "Identify every banking institution at which you currently hold an account."

Requests for admission are pretty similar to interrogatories. One party sends a list of statements to the other party, which they then admit or deny. Doesn't sound particularly useful, does it? Surprisingly, it can be a good way to establish relevant facts in the case. There's incentive for a party to answer requests for admission because any questions that are unanswered or ignored will be presumed to be admitted, which can lead to very serious consequences. Imagine a party ignoring the question: "Admit that you drink at least a case of beer every night and smoke crack cocaine in front of the children." Inadvertently admitting a question like that wouldn't exactly help your custody case, unless you happened to be tried in a parallel universe.

One of my favorite tools of discovery is subpoenaing information from a third party. Say a party is self-employed and insists that his or her income is twenty thousand dollars a year. If I have a pretty good idea that's not actually the case, I'll probably issue a subpoena to their bank for all their banking records, and issue another subpoena to a few of their key customers to prove that their income isn't what they say it is. The added bonus of this tactic is that you're sometimes able to discredit the other party by proving that the sworn answer they previously submitted in an interrogatory or document request was not truthful. It tends to hurt a party's credibility on the witness stand when they're confronted with their own conflicting information.

Finally, the deposition is a very powerful tool that can be used when a case is likely to go to trial. In a deposition, the deposing attorney sits at a table across from the person being deposed and interrogates the person for several hours. At best, a skilled deponent can dig deep into the facts on a wide variety of topics and often receives answers from the opposing party that can change the course of the entire case. At worst, the attorney is given an advantage at trial because they gather a feel for how the person will testify, can better read their mannerisms, and can predict the answers they'll likely give to specific questions. The deposition is always recorded by a court reporter and often videotaped so the attorney can study it later. Between the court reporters time, the attorney's prep time, deposition time, and time spent reviewing the transcript, depositions quickly become extremely expensive so they are usually reserved for only the most contentious of cases.

It might seem counterintuitive to someone unfamiliar with the law, but the point of all this information exchange is to ensure everyone has a full picture of the relevant case circumstances and is on the same page at trial. True, it does make for a lot less excitement and drama than you'd see on TV, but it also makes for a much cleaner practice of the law. We'll leave the "gotchas" to Matlock and McBeal for now.

PART TWO
Chapter Five

Expert Evaluations

My personal mantra when preparing for trial? Quality over quantity. Quality of evidence trumps quantity of evidence almost every time. In my experience, there's nothing better than submitting an evaluation from an expert who's made a careful and thorough determination on an issue. If the expert is credible, has a good reputation, and can coherently explain their recommendation to the court, it's pretty likely that the expert's advice will be closely followed.

A few months ago while I was sitting in the gallery waiting for my case to be called, another attorney made a reference during his argument to the court that the judge "rubber stamped" custody evaluation recommendations—meaning when the experts submitted recommendations to the court, the judge approved the recommendations without a second thought. The judge did not appreciate the comment and the attorney had his foot in his mouth for the rest of the hearing, but there was more than a hint of truth to what he said. Good expert evaluations can pack a lot of punch with a judge.

Like a box of chocolates or a brand new Lego set, evaluations come in a lot of different shapes and sizes. Some are court ordered and some are undertaken voluntarily. Some are done by neutral evaluators, and some are done by evaluators who are anything but. Some also hold more weight in court than others. A judge is more likely to be persuaded by the opinion of an evaluator who was agreed upon by both parties, is unbiased, and is recognized as a leader in their field, than someone who was selected specifically to serve one party's interest. (If only politics were the same way, right?)

Different evaluations are handy for different kinds of

cases, and some cases will require many at one time. The types of evaluations I tend to use most frequently are custody evaluations, vocational evaluations, medical evaluations, business valuations, and property appraisals. In my practice we mostly use neutral evaluations that are agreed to and paid for by each of the parties equally. In addition to costing less than each side hiring their own expert, neutral evaluations tend to carry more weight with the court. They're also often a good tool in settling cases before trial, as they provide both sides with an idea of how a judge would likely rule on each particular issue.

I deal with more custody and parenting time evaluations than any other kind by far. So much of what's presented in a custody hearing is subjective he-said she-said evidence. There just aren't a lot of reliable, objective records to prove which parent is "better." There's no points system or parent trading card statistics keeping track of who read bedtime stories to little Johnny every night, and who pays more attention to reality TV than darling Janey's piano practice. Without the report of a neutral expert who's taken the time to speak extensively with the parents and relevant third parties like teachers and relatives, courts would be forced to base custody decisions on two competing personal stories. Instead, when custody is at issue many judges require the parents to cooperate with a custody evaluator who will delve into their lives for several months and author a fairly extensive report that addresses each of the "best interest" custody factors.[12]

The report usually ends with a recommendation regarding both custody labels as well as a proposed parenting time schedule. While my colleague's off-the-cuff remark that judges "rubber stamp" these reports is not completely true, they do give parties a pretty clear idea of what the court is likely to order. Of

---

12 Custody determinations in Minnesota are based upon a determination of what serves the children's' best interests. Minnesota Statute §518.17 lists the 13 "best interest" factors that are taken into consideration by the court.

course, every attorney encounters evaluations that are poorly written or are not at all favorable towards their client one in a while. Cross-examining the evaluator and attempting to poke holes in their evaluation is sometimes the best option in those situations.

In cases where property values are at issue, an expert appraisal of the property's market value tends to carry a lot of weight. Most people don't have a very good grip on how much their home is actually worth, and I handle a lot of cases where each party has a vastly different number in mind. Hiring a professional real estate appraiser to settle the debate usually makes for a better case than the wife claiming "the neighbor's house sold for three-hundred thousand and ours is much nicer" while the husband poo-poos the tacky vinyl floors and shoddy paint job. Same thing goes for small business ownership and valuation of collectibles like artwork and old cars. Even things that seem to have an obvious value, like a pension, are more complicated than you'd think. Hiring an actuary to determine the present value of a retirement account can really help clarify what assets are on the table.[13]

When earning ability is at issue, usually in a case involving spousal maintenance, "employing" a vocational evaluator is a useful trick. This often occurs when one party is unemployed, or under-employed, and claims that they need ongoing support from the other party to get by. The party on the hook for maintenance can have a vocational expert meet with the ex and review their qualifications in light of the current job market. The vocational evaluator will then prepare a report stating what the person is likely to earn, what additional training or education they may need, and how long it will likely take before they can

---

13 The value of your retirement account may not be what it seems –
    particularly if it is the type of account that can't be accessed until you reach
    a certain age, or one that pays out a monthly benefit, an actuary must make
    a determination of its "present value" so that it can be properly divided on
    the date of the divorce.

get on their feet financially. In the case of a party who claims that they're unable to work because of an injury, requesting an independent medical evaluation might also be necessary.

Along with the information exchanged during the discovery process, evaluations help clear the total picture and give both the court and the parties a better idea of the realities of the case. Evaluators are sort of like the Windex of the legal world. If the specifics in a case seem foggy, spray a little evaluation action up on there. As with a lot of things in the divorce process (and unlike Windex), they're not often cheap, but they're almost always worth it.

Chapter Six

Last-Ditch Effort: The pretrial/settlement conference

Status update! You've completed the initial hearing, gone through mediation or neutral evaluation, and finished the discovery process. Temporary motions have been taken care of and everybody is ready to go to trial and get this show on the road. Time to burn rubber and put it all behind you, right? Not so fast, Jeff Gordon. There's still a few minutes left on your Stair Master routine. The next step in a divorce or custody case is the pretrial conference, also known in some counties as the settlement conference or the moderated settlement conference. No matter what the name, the purpose of the conference is to appear one last time before your trial date, give the court an update of what issues are still at stake, and attempt to negotiate an agreement face-to-face.

Since there are no contested issues to be decided or legal arguments to be made, the hearing itself is not particularly difficult. The judge will want to know what issues remain contested should there be a trial, and usually asks why everything hasn't been settled already. You'll definitely be left with the impression that the court wants to avoid seeing you again at trial. Don't worry, you don't have spinach in your teeth or something, that's just the way the system works.

In some counties, the pretrial is set up as a "calendar call" (or "cattle call," as attorneys like to refer to it). At a calendar call, you sit in the courtroom with ten or twenty other people who also have pre-trials scheduled that day, and each of you gets a few minutes to update the judge. In other counties you're assigned a specific time block, sometimes several hours, during which you're expected to negotiate to any remaining issues with the judge available on-call to answer any questions. Some judges are willing to assert themselves into the negotiation process more than others. And some are even willing to give a pretty strong indication of how they might rule on a specific issue at trial. Though the judge's comments are off the record, they tend to help settle cases even if one party doesn't like what they heard.

A new type of hearing being used in some metro counties is the moderated settlement conference. This is a lot like the early neutral evaluation we talked about a few chapters ago. With the help of an experienced moderator who has been chosen from a list of qualified court-approved attorneys, everyone meets at the courthouse and makes one last-ditch effort to hammer out a deal. The settlement moderator helps guide the process, gives their professional opinion, and works to keep things focused. Both parties must pay the moderator's hourly rate for this conference; however, it's set by the court, so it is usually pretty reasonable, and always far less expensive than going to trial.

Since ENE wasn't successful in producing an agreement it's hard to believe that a moderated settlement conference would be, right? The theory of moderated settlement is that even if it didn't work the first time another try is still worthwhile, especially now that discovery has occurred and all the facts are in the open. The difference in location between the ENE, which takes place at an attorney's office, and the moderated settlement conference, which takes place in the court house, is significant enough to have an impact as well.

The advantage of holding the settlement conference at the courthouse is that the judge assigned to the case is available to answer any questions and provide guidance on sticking points. If the parties reach an agreement, they can put it on the record right then and there instead of having to wait for the next court date. In my experience, there's something about physically being in the courthouse that tends to make people take negotiations more seriously than they do in an office building, too. Maybe we can just chalk it up to inherent reverence for any man or woman in a robe.

The pretrial is usually the last time the parties will get to meet and negotiate a settlement before the trial date. Even if a full settlement isn't reached, it's important to resolve as many issues as possible. It's much easier (and cheaper) to prepare for a trial that solely deals with spousal maintenance than it is to prepare to litigate every aspect of someone's former marriage and financial future. Judges don't use the strong-arm technique to encourage settlement just because they don't feel like sitting through a three-day divorce trial. It's because they know that the agreements parties reach on their own are almost always better than what the court must come up with instead.

PART TWO
Chapter Seven

The wait is (almost) over – Trial day

Now that you have been reading this book for a bit, hopefully enjoying and relating to what I have to say, it's fair to say that we've built a mini-relationship and you can trust in what I tell you, right? I hate to potentially ruin this hard earned trust, but I have to admit that I lied to you last chapter. Remember when I said that the pre-trial conference was your last-ditch chance to hash out the differences and settle the case? Not necessarily true. Many cases settle on the day of trial – in fact, more cases that are scheduled for trial actually settle at the courthouse than actually go through with the trial.

When you show up to the courthouse with exhibits, witnesses, and nerves all raring to go, you're going to be disappointed at how the day likely starts. Many judges will not start by swearing in witnesses or by hearing opening statements, but instead start the day by again ordering the parties to go outside the courtroom and work on reaching a resolution to the issues. Sometimes it is successful, sometimes it isn't, but at this point in the process, everyone knows exactly what is at stake, knows what is going to be presented as evidence, what each witness is going to say, what arguments are going to be made, and has an idea what the judge is fairly likely to decide. Unless the case is really unusual or complex, or one side persists on digging their heels in, there usually isn't a real good reason for a trial to take place.

That being said, trials are sometimes ultimately necessary, and they do sometimes actually take place. One of the big things you are paying your attorney for is courtroom experience, right? While it is extremely important to have an attorney through every other step of the process, this is the one part that is quite impossible for you to handle on your own. It takes a lot of education and experience for any attorney to master things like evidence introduction, objections, cross-examination techniques, and presenting a persuasive story through direct and cross examination. There are no juries in family law, and the rules can't be bent for people proceeding without an attorney, so you only get one chance to present your version of the story to the judge. For example, if the other attorney is making objectionable statements or lines of questioning, you don't get a minute (or even more than a split-second) to consider how to object and why - you just have to know what you're doing, or I can promise that the trial won't go well.

The trial itself usually starts with brief opening statements by each side. Some attorneys choose to skip these statements, as the judge has a pretty good idea of the issues in the case and each party's point of view beforehand. I personally usually like to make a very brief opening statement if given the opportunity to do so – so long as we're all here, why pass up an opportunity to express your point of view and set the tone for the case? Before any of the exciting stuff starts, preliminary matters, such as motions in limine (last minute rulings requested by either party) and stipulations to things like the admissibility of exhibits or expert testimony will also be addressed. The judge will also likely give the parties an attorneys a speech about courtroom decorum and how to speak so that the court reporter can properly transcribe the entire proceeding.

After the opening statement, the petitioner gets to call their witnesses, and the petitioner's attorney questions them under oath. This can be a lot trickier than it seems – except for very limited circumstances, questions can't be leading ("Isn't it true that you take the children to their doctor's appointments"), but also can't be too vague ("tell me about your relationship with Johnny") Proper foundation must be laid for every question, and questions that call for hearsay must be avoided ("what did

Johnny tell you on Thursday?"). The respondent's attorney gets an opportunity to cross-examine the witnesses after the direct examination is finished, which simply means that it is the other side's turn to question that witness. Unlike with direct examination, leading questions ("Isn't it true"-type questions) are allowed, and even encouraged. This is the respondent's turn to poke holes in the petitioner's story and even damage their credibility if they can point out some inconsistencies in their tale.

Once the petitioner is finished presenting their witnesses and exhibits, the roles flip-flop and it's now the respondent's turn to tell their side of the story, and the petitioner's time to cross examine. After this all takes place, which I've obviously completely over-simplified to keep this chapter from being hundreds of pages long, each side gets to make a closing argument, which is often actually done in writing and not in person at the courthouse. After that, everyone packs up and goes home. What? The Judge doesn't bang a gavel and say "you get the kids, you get the house..."? Sorry Charlie.

Before the judge can make a ruling on the case, each party usually submits their proposed order, along with a memorandum of law regarding any complicated issue that the judge may need educated about. Basically, this is their opportunity to tell the court exactly what they think the final divorce decree should look like. Helpful hint – the judge is more likely to agree with you if your proposal is a reasonable compromise and less likely to sign off on a proposed order that gives you the proverbial gold mine and your ex the shaft.

Once the trial date is finished and closing arguments and proposed orders have been submitted, the court needs some time to think everything over and issue a final decision. You didn't think the waiting game was quite over yet, did you? The court has 90 days to issue their final order, and usually takes almost every one of them. Then, and only then is the divorce process finally over, and you can get on with your new life.

Except, of course, unless one party decides to appeal the decision – but that's a story for a whole 'nother book.

PART THREE
Chapter One

Custody and parenting time

Since I'm a lawyer and lawyers basically can't say anything without a caveat, let me start the chapter with this disclaimer: Child custody issues are so complex and varied that this entire book could focus solely on them and still only scratch the surface. I'll do my best to make like Hemingway and get straight to the point, but just imagine this chapter is less like an intricate blueprint of custody issues and more like a 10,000 foot flyover view.

There's one phrase you're going to hear over and over when dealing with custody issues, and for good reason. "Best interests of the children" is the most vital takeaway I can give you. Not only is it an incredibly important mantra to live by when making decisions during your divorce, it's also something you're likely going to hear repeatedly from your attorney, the judge, and anyone else involved in the custody determination process. So what exactly does the term custody determination mean? Let's take a minute to parse it out. The answer isn't quite as simple as you might think.

In Minnesota, there are two custody labels to be determined: legal custody and physical custody. Legal custody refers to the right to have input on your child's major life decisions– things such as religious upbringing, important medical issues, and where to attend school. Except under extreme circumstances, it's very common for parents to share "joint" legal custody. Physical custody refers to the child's primary residence. This can also be shared jointly, though it is somewhat more common for one parent to be the sole physical custodian. Remember – custody can be shared "jointly" or can be "sole" – there is no such thing as "fifty-fifty" custody, though I hear that term almost daily in my practice. There also tends to be lot of misinformation out there that the physical custody label determines child support – it doesn't.[14]

Guess what legal standard is used to make an initial determination of physical custody? Hopefully you paid attention earlier and are mouthing the all-important words, "best interests of the children," right now. In Minnesota, there are thirteen factors defined by statute that guide the court in determining the children's best interests.[15] The court looks to answer such questions like, "Who was the child's primary caretaker during the marriage?", "Does either parent have serious mental health or chemical abuse concerns?", "Does one parent have a more stable living situation than the other?" and if the children are older, "What arrangements do the children prefer?" All of the factors listed in the statute have to be considered, so the court can't use just one to make a final determination. As much as some parents want to say "my ex is on a first name basis with everyone at the local liquor store, so I should get custody of the kids," it's a little more complicated than that. Drinking problems are definitely relevant, but if the other parent is, for example, a transient felon who has been minimally involved in the children's' lives, the nightly six-pack might just be outweighed by other factors.

Before I move on from the "best interest" talk, a common mistake I see from both clients and attorneys alike is spending too much time railing on the other parent and not enough time talking about their own relationship with the kids. The vast majority of cases I handle involve happy, healthy, well-adjusted children. Going through some custody cases, which sometimes feel like an amateur version of Celebrity Roast, it's hard not to question how the kids turned out so well. While I do bring up

---

14 Under the prior child support laws, the physical custody label did play in to the child support calculation, but this hasn't been the case in many years – this probably explains the source of the confusion.

15 See Minnesota Statute §518.17 for a complete list of the thirteen "best interest" factors.

concerns about the other parent if necessary, I tend to focus more on the positive qualities of my clients' relationships with their children. This might include special activities they take part in together, their involvement in school and community life, and even special nicknames they might have for each other. As scary as they might seem, judges are human too, and I'm pretty sure hearing nothing but the negatives gets pretty tiring pretty fast. Even old stick-in-the-mud Judge Judy has a soft spot underneath.

When it comes down to it on a day-to-day basis, the actual parenting time schedule is more important that the label of physical custody. I'm not suggesting that the custody label doesn't carry weight, but where the children actually spend their time is really what matters, right?[16] People like to ask me what a typical parenting time schedule is, and—again with the lawyer thing—I can never really give a straight answer. Some common schedules I see involve rotating every other week, one parent having most weekdays and the other having every other weekend, one parent having the majority of the school year and the other the majority of the summer, and even "5-2-2-5" schedules.[17] Parenting time schedules can be written any way the parties like, keeping in mind that they should serve the (say it with me now) best interests of the children. For example, in a case where two parents live a distance apart, a weekly rotating schedule probably isn't going to work for school-aged children.

Many times in high-conflict situations, one or both parents tend to want to deny all parenting time to the other. At least here in Minnesota, that isn't usually a feasible proposition. As many studies and most judges will tell you, children almost always benefit from having a relationship with both of their

---

16 Although it doesn't have a ton of impact on day-to-day life, the physical custody label can be extremely important, however, when attempting to change the parenting time schedule later on down the line.

17 5-2-2-5 schedules create equal parenting time for each parent, where parent A gets 5 days with the kids, followed by 2 days for parent B, then 2 for parent A, then 5 for parent B.

parents, even if one is not an ideal role model. While the law here isn't set up to push people towards equally split parenting time, it does provide that each parent should get at least twenty five percent of overnights with the children unless there are extenuating circumstances.

The age of the children is yet another factor to take into account. As much as we'd like to buy our kids one wardrobe when they're born and be done with, trying to squeeze a teenager into a onesie isn't really going to work. There's no such thing as a one size fits all when it comes to children, and the same applies to parenting time. An appropriate schedule for an eight-month-old is very different from that for an eight-year-old.

One of the first things any parent going through a custody dispute should check out is the "Parental Guide to Making Child Focused Decisions." It's available on the Internet for free, and I guarantee that both your attorney and the judge deciding your case are very familiar with it. The booklet describes different developmental needs for children of different ages, and includes recommendations for parenting time for each stage. For example, infants need predictability and consistency and may experience separation anxiety if away from the primary parent for long periods. Thus, the recommendation for very young children is to have frequent, but short, parenting time for the non-custodial parent, which generally does not include overnights.

If you had to make a life-changing decision about your kid's physical health you wouldn't go to just anybody with an MD behind their name, you'd seek out an actual specialist. So when it comes to making life-changing decisions about your family's emotional well-being, you really need to work with lawyer who knows what they're doing. Just like cancer needs an oncologist, custody and parenting time issues need a family law attorney. Even if parents are committed to working together to do what's best for the kids, this is one area where playing amateur attorney is a really bad idea. If simply reading this extremely generalized chapter left your brain feeling boggled, imagine trying to navigate the ins and outs of your specific case. Child custody is an extremely complex area of law with many nuances. Each one can affect your family in immeasurable ways, so you want to make absolutely sure everything is done right the first time. Remember how I told you "best interests of the children" is the most important takeaway of this chapter? Well, I have another one for you: "Get thee to a good attorney, stat!"

PART TWO
Chapter Two

Child Support

You don't need a perfectly coiffed TV anchor to deliver the not-so-breaking news that having kids is really darn expensive. You just need to look at your credit card bill. All the kids that I've met tend to like to eat, wear clothes, ruin said clothes, play expensive sports, sleep in their own bedroom, and get chauffeured to and from their best friend's ninja themed birthday party, all on mom's and dad's dime. So, what happens when one parent spends the majority of time with the children and has to foot the bill for the chicken fingers, Baby Gap, and minivan payments? Usually, the other parent has to reimburse them for some of these expenses through the child support process. Most people can agree that some settling of the tab makes sense, it's when you try to decide just how much of that tab the other parent is paying and what exactly it's going toward that things get dicey.

The mechanics of figuring basic child support in Minnesota are actually pretty easy, especially if there's no dispute over how much each parent earns. The Minnesota Department of Human Services provides a handy online calculator that most of the judges and attorneys I know rely on to help determine child support. Go to http://childsupportcalculator.dhs.state.mn.us/ Calculator.aspx and take a look around. There are boxes to input information for "Parent A" (the parent with less parenting time) and "Parent B" (the primary parent). Type in the relevant information, like number of children, monthly income, medical insurance expenses, and daycare expenses. Click on calculate, and a worksheet that shows the guideline child support amount magically appears. Not quite as thrilling as the magic Cinderella's

Fairy Godmother used to turn a pumpkin into a carriage, but most fairytales don't end with Cinderella and the Prince negotiating child support down at the courthouse either.

Let's try working through a totally made up, not at all lifted from the bowels of TMZ.com, example. Imagine a couple—we'll call them Kris and Kim—who have two children together and decide to get a divorce. The children end up with Kris (Parent B), but Kim (Parent A) spends time with the kids every other weekend and overnight every Wednesday. According to line fifteen of the form, this puts her in the "between twelve and forty-five percent parenting time" bracket. Kris plays for a minor-league basketball team and makes $7,800 per month. Kim works at K-Mart as a fashion designer and earns $4,900 per month. Neither have any non-joint children, and neither are ordered to pay spousal maintenance to anyone. Kris carries the children on his medical and dental policy at the cost of $250 per month and pays $1,200 a month for daycare. Plugging these numbers into the formula, our magic wand tells us that Kim owes Kris a total of $1,377 a month.

To demonstrate how income can affect the child support calculation, let's reverse incomes and give Kris the job at K-Mart and Kim the basketball job, while keeping everything else the same. The total support owed from Kim to Kris in that case turns out to be $2,154 per month. Quite a bit higher than before, even though the parties aggregate income is the same, because in this scenario the kids live with the parent who earns less.

Let's add a few more variables to see how they affect things. Keeping Kris at K-Mart and Kim playing basketball, let's assume that Kim was ordered to pay her ex-husband, Kanye, spousal maintenance of $4,500 per month. This amount is effectively deducted from her income, which would then drop her child support total to $1,145.

Just for fun, let's go back and remove that spousal maintenance obligation, but assume that Kris and Kim split their parenting time equally. That results in a monthly obligation of $1,231, which is a far cry from the $2,154 that it would be otherwise.

Confused yet? Well you can relax and unbunch those undies. Calculating child support isn't nearly as complicated as my scenarios above might make it seem. Overall, it's mostly a matter of figuring out exactly which variables apply to your situation, plugging those numbers into the calculator, and getting the result. But if child support really is just a bunch of equations and magic calculators, why are there so many disputes about it? Can't some computer just take care of everything? Well, as fun as the above examples were, I guess it's possible I may have oversimplified the processm a bit.

In the real world, people have names that start with letters other than K and not everyone earns a consistent salary. Some people make varying or seasonal income, some earn tips that may or may not be reported as income, some occasionally get overtime pay, some may be self-employed and understating their income—there's an extreme amount of variability. But that's not all! What about money that goes toward taxes or a retirement plan? What if one person is living off of student loans or a trust fund? What about someone who used to make good money, but is now voluntarily working part-time or is unemployed? What about someone who stays home because their new spouse is loaded? Not so easy to plug a number into the calculator and wave the magic wand now, is it?

Minnesota Statute §518A.29 defines what is and is not counted as income for child support purposes. For the most part, if you receive any kind of money it's going to be considered for child support. Some exceptions may include overtime pay, pay from a second job, child support received from another person, and any income your new spouse earns if you have remarried. In fact, if it can be demonstrated that you aren't earning as much as you should be because of voluntary unemployment or underemployment, income can be imputed to you so that your "potential income" will be used to determine child support instead of the actual figure. Guess that lemonade and hammock is going to have to wait, eh?

Income figures aren't the only potential gray areas in calculating child support. As you saw in my earlier examples, the amount of parenting time that each party has with the child can make a huge difference in the bottom line support. Usually parenting time percentages are simply calculated by number of overnights spent at each parent's house, but there are alternate methods of calculating, too.

It's important to remember that the bottom line amount of child support to be paid determined by the calculator isn't set in stone. It's a guideline calculation, but it can be deviated from, either upwards or downwards, under the right circumstances.[18] Not all children have the same financial needs so the law allows for some variability from the guidelines, though most Judges and Magistrates tend to stick pretty close to the book in my experience.

Now that you have a basic child support amount figured out, what about the health insurance and day care expenses for the kids? Fortunately the Legislature, in their infinite wisdom, did not forget those costs. They are factored into the net child support calculation (remember the boxes asking for the amount paid for child care and medical and dental insurance on the online calculator form?) and are included in the total amount. They are effectively split so that each parent pays a percentage of the expense roughly in line with their income level as compared to the other parent. So, to oversimplify it for you, if one parent makes $1,000 a month and the other makes $9,000, the higher earning parent will pay 90% of the costs, and the lower earning parent will pay the remaining 10%. The lower paying parent

_____

18   See Minnesota Statute § 518A.43 for a list of factors that allow a deviation from the guideline child support amount.

simply reimburses the higher paying parent for their percentage of the costs through the support system, rather than dealing with the insurance company or daycare provider directly.

I could go on forever about the myriad of additional child support topics – enforcement of child support, collection of support, calculating past support, birthing and confinement expenses, child support contempt. I'm sure you'd have a real ball reading about them, but I'll spare you the sordid details for now. This chapter has been all about bottom lines, and the bottom line I'll leave you with is this: except in the most simple of circumstances, talk to an attorney who knows what they're doing and has handled child support matters before. In general, child support is a pretty complicated thing, and when children are involved it's not worth taking the risk of a magic wand. A competent attorney will help you get the amount right, get it paid easily, and will be able to modify it if and when circumstances change. Little Timmy is a growing boy and those Nikes he's rocking are just so last season, you know?

PART THREE
Chapter Three

Spousal Maintenance

If there is a magic calculator that determines child support guidelines like the one we looked at in the last chapter, then there must be one to determine spousal maintenance too, right? Ah, it's sweet of you to think so, really. Unfortunately my friend, you are far, far away from the truth. Spousal maintenance —formerly known as "alimony"—is one of the most complicated, unpredictable, and frequently changing issues in divorce law. So take that lovely image of a spousal maintenance calculator and throw it out your rose-tinted window.

The court's decision on the same exact case can vary wildly from county to county, week to week, and especially judge to judge. While there are factors the court has to take into consideration when deciding if maintenance is appropriate and what the terms are if ordered, there's so much judicial discretion and constant development in case law that it's nearly impossible to predict with any certainty.[19] This is one area where your attorney's experience in a particular courtroom (or their willingness to consult with colleagues who have spent time in a particular courtroom) really makes a difference. Understanding and preparing for the unique nuances of a courtroom, like the tendencies of certain judges for example, can make a big difference in the outcome of your case. That being said, there are some factors every court takes into consideration in a maintenance case and understanding how those relate to your specific situation is a good first step.

No matter what the situation is, every divorce case must

---

19 "Case law" refers to decisions made by the Court of Appeals and Supreme Court, which impact decisions made by the district courts, who are obligated to follow the guidance the higher courts provide.

determine whether spousal maintenance should be awarded, and if so, how much and in what way. The first and most important question is whether spousal maintenance is even at issue in the case. If the parties make roughly equal incomes, have only been married a short time, or just aren't requesting maintenance, then stop here. No need to get further entangled in the web of spousal support if it isn't going to be ordered in the first place.

In the event that spousal maintenance is at issue, a myriad of delightful questions arise. What happens if the party receiving maintenance remarries or the person paying maintenance passes away? Would it make more sense to pay a one-time lump sum instead of a monthly payment? And what tax consequences or benefits result from the award? Can the monthly maintenance award be used as income when buying a new home? These are the kinds of questions that keep me up at night, tossing and turning in my Star Wars jammies, so I'll do my best to shed some lawyerly light on this nightmare of a topic.

From a simplified standpoint, spousal maintenance is at issue if one spouse isn't able to meet their reasonable financial needs on their own and the other has the ability to help them. Of course, what is "reasonable" varies from family to family, so the court takes into consideration the standard of living that was established during the marriage. Though it might be tempting to try, it's probably not reasonable for a spouse who lived in a studio apartment to ask for enough maintenance to afford a new Lake Minnetonka beachfront condo. Conversely, the spouse who's lived in the penthouse for the past twenty years can't reasonably be expected to now hightail it to the proverbial doghouse. That being said, the courts understand that it's more expensive for two people to live separately than together, so it's not realistic for either party to expect the full marital standard of living to be maintained after the divorce—especially not on their ex's dime.

Now that we've got some vague idea about the purpose of spousal maintenance, let's talk about duration. If maintenance is ordered, how long should it be provided? Spousal support can either come in the form of a temporary payment, permanent payment, or a lump sum. Temporary, or rehabilitative, support only lasts for a set number of years and is often ordered in situations where the lower-earning spouse needs some time to become self-supporting. A common example is a parent who left the workforce to stay home with children, and now needs education, training, or just some time to re-climb the corporate ladder before they can reasonably make it on their own. Some attorneys will try to tell you that the length of the maintenance always lasts for half of the length of the marriage. For example, five years of maintenance would be awarded for a ten year marriage. Don't listen to those goons.

As with everything in this chapter, that's a serious oversimplification and is often far from accurate. Another, more realistic approach, is to estimate how long it will take to obtain the education, training, and experience necessary to earn the big bucks. Temporary spousal maintenance awards can even be "stepped-down" over time to gradually decrease in proportion with the rise of expected earning potential. Watch out for these step down awards or any award that lasts less than three years, though—there are some complicated IRS rules involved that can catch you off guard if you aren't careful.

Permanent maintenance, on the other hand, doesn't specify a set number of months or years that support will continue. It also doesn't actually mean that it will be paid permanently. A more accurate label for permanent maintenance would be "until something changes" maintenance. For example, if the paying spouse loses their job and can't find another one that pays as well, it should change. If the paying spouse reaches a reasonable retirement age and each spouse has reasonably equal retirement assets, it's probably a good bet that maintenance will end. If the spouse receiving maintenance suddenly lands their dream job and starts making big dolla dolla billz, time to end that permanent maintenance pronto. Permanent is a pretty heavy term, and in this case it's also a pretty loose one.

So, now that we've got that covered let's get to the numbers. How many Benjamins is this actually going to cost you? In the last three months alone I've handled cases involving spousal maintenance as low as $200 per month and as high as $6,800 per month. The numbers are truly all over the board, and there's no set guideline for judges or attorneys to follow in figuring it out. One popular method to figure out a starting point is to simply split the kitty for a while. Take each spouses income, put it in a pot, and split the total in half.[20] Things get a little trickier if one spouse has higher reasonable living expenses than the other. Maybe one has to pay out of pocket for health insurance, is stuck with the marital house financed at 17% interest, or went to law school and has $140,000 of student loans to pay down each month (not that I would know anything about that). Realistically, it's all up to the individual judge to determine what they think is a reasonable amount, and each judge's view of what's reasonable is different.

Taxes are yet another important thing to keep in mind when dealing with spousal maintenance. Maintenance is usually taxable as income for the person receiving it, and a tax deduction for the person who's paying it. Since the person paying is generally earning a higher income, and thus taxed at a higher rate than the payee, you can actually *save* money through a maintenance award. For example, if Bill pays Sue $20,000 in maintenance in a year, it's taxed at Sue's tax rate of 10% instead of Bill's tax rate of 30%, even though Bill earned the money.

---

20 Of course, niggling details like "potential income" for an unemployed or underemployed spouse, and the tax consequences of the maintenance payment have to be taken into consideration, but that is for the advanced course.

Every dollar that stays in your pocket and out of the IRS's grabby paws is a win, right?

Spousal maintenance usually ends if either party passes away or the recipient remarries, though the parties can agree to modify those rules. It's also pretty common to require a party who has to pay spousal support to carry life insurance to cover their obligation, just in case something happens. Any award of spousal maintenance can later be modified by the court unless the parties agree on what is called a *Karon* waiver, which sets the award in stone and takes away the court's power to later change it —no matter what.

If you hadn't gleaned already, the moral of this straight-to-TV story is that spousal maintenance is tricky. So tricky, in fact, that some lawyers don't even really understand it. Those who do are indispensable, and though you're probably tired of hearing me say it, you need to talk to one of them if you want to effectively navigate your way through this tough issue. Spousal maintenance is a lot like a carnival funhouse, except with all the mazes and none of the fun. A wrong turn could lead you into the grips of a creepy clown, but the right attorney will get you out safe on the other side with your cotton candy still in hand.

PART THREE
Chapter Four

Property division

Contrary to popular belief and Hollywood movies, splitting up all the stuff is actually the simplest part of many divorces. It's the rules about how to split it that are difficult for people to come to terms with. First, let me define what I mean by "stuff". There are tangible possessions, like cars, furniture, rare paintings, and stamp collections. And then there are the less tangible financial things, like bank accounts, retirement savings, and even debt. Basically, stuff includes everything either party owns except for real estate, which we'll deal with later. Most people who've been married for any length of time don't realize just how much stuff there is until it's time to split it up. Open up your nearest "junk drawer" and have a look. Though the flashlights, rubber bands, and two-year-old pieces of Play-Doh you keep in there aren't up for dispute, it's a pretty good visual representation of how many things we accumulate over the years.

In Minnesota, property must be split "fairly and equitably", which generally means equally.[21] The easiest and most common way to do this is to make a list of everything of value (no, that doesn't include every individual piece of Tupperware) and divide it up in such a way that Husband walks away with the same amount of "stuff" as Wife does. That doesn't necessarily mean dividing everything in half. For example, if Husband gets the collection of original Picassos, maybe Wife gets the retirement savings to make up for it. Many

---

21 Sometimes it is "fair and equitable" for one party to get more of the stuff than the other – for example I had a case a few years ago in which the Husband (unbeknownst to the Wife) got scammed in to sending hundreds of thousands of dollars to Internet "acquaintances". The debt that created was given to him alone, because it's only fair!

times, one party ends up with a little more stuff than the other, which means that they have to make an "equalizer" payment to the other person to even it out. I try to avoid that situation. Usually a little creativity is needed to divide up everything so both parties walk away close enough to equal.

So far, this sounds pretty easy, right? Well, yeah, in a basic sense it is. The tricky part, and what people sometimes struggle to wrap their minds around, is what's considered marital "stuff" and what's not. Generally speaking, in Minnesota, whatever was acquired during the time of the marriage is marital property regardless of whose name it's in.[22] That means that the retirement plan you earned during the marriage, or at least the portion of it that was earned during the marriage, is both of yours. The credit card debt that your spouse racked up with their addiction to fine chocolates and cigars is both of yours as well. Even the business that you started from scratch and built into a multi-billion dollar corporation – yep, if it was started during the marriage then again, it's both of yours.

Some things are naturally trickier than others to divide. Household goods and furnishings are pretty easy. I once had a client who turned splitting the household goods into a game with their soon-to-be ex. They each got a few sheets of stickers and took turns placing their color sticker on what they wanted. Sounds like a scene from a sitcom, right? Of course, some couples are more fit for TV dramas than sitcoms and have a harder time being amicable. In my experience there's no quicker way to annoy a judge than prattling on about who gets Aunt Mary's antique china set and who gets the everyday IKEA plates.

Surprisingly, financial accounts are actually fairly easy to split as well. Any "liquid" account, such as checking, savings, and some investment accounts, can simply be divided equally.

---

22 The most common exceptions are "pre-marital" property (something that one party owned prior to the marriage), gifts to one party only, and inheritances.

Retirement accounts and pensions are a little trickier, as they need a separate court document called a "qualified domestic relations order" to divide up the account, which often isn't accessible by either party until reaching a certain age even after division. Debt accounts are slightly tougher. A divorce decree can certainly order Husband to be responsible for the Citibank Visa in Wife's name, but if he decides against making a payment in the future, guess how much Citibank is going to care what a Minnesota divorce decree states? They're still going to go after the Wife for the balance of the account, and her only remedy is to turn around and sue her now ex-husband for what she's out. For this reason, it's almost always advisable to divide the debt so the person whose name it's in keeps it whenever possible.

Sometimes an expert opinion is needed to determine the value of some of the "stuff". That commissioned oil painting of Colonel Meow Meow might look like a priceless masterpiece to you, but if your spouse thinks it belongs in the kitty litter you're going to run into some issues. If the parties can't agree on how much something is reasonably worth they need an outsider to have the final say. Expert valuations are often performed for cars, businesses, collections, and jewelry, among other things. Even the "present value" of retirement accounts and pensions needs to be determined by an expert to figure out how much they're truly worth.[23]

Once everyone has an idea of what's in the marital "hotchpot" and what it's all worth, the next step is figuring out who gets what and how to make sure the bottom line is pretty close to equal. On paper this should be fairly easy, but like everything in a divorce, it isn't always so. For example, if I were going through a divorce, I'd be much more interested in keeping my mechanics toolset than I would the fancy furniture we've

---

23 An actuary can calculate, based upon a formula that takes life expectancy, inflation, and other considerations in to account, an estimate of the "present value" of the account. It's pretty complicated stuff, definitely best left to the actuaries themselves to explain.

accumulated. What if my wife doesn't want the furniture either, but also wants the tools? Maybe because she wants to get into mechanics, or maybe because she just wants to be a jerk. Maybe then I decide to go after her entire shoe collection as retribution for the tool thing, and the whole property division exercise spirals out of control. The goal, obviously, is to avoid this. My wife doesn't have any need for a cylinder hone and I don't have any need for size eight Jimmy Choo's (though size ten would be a different story). Only a really exceptional person would find the spiteful sense of revenge worth losing a bunch of stuff they actually want and gaining a bunch of crap that they don't.

I like to refer to the process of splitting the stuff as horse trading. Once everybody knows what's on the table and what isn't, and once everybody has a good sense of what they want and what the other person wants, it's time to deal. One boat for two couches. One retirement plan for all the credit card debt. As sick as it sounds, given that both parties often feel like they're starting their lives over anyway, the property division is kind of like a huge garage sale. And like any good garage sale, the goal is to walk away with the best stuff in your fanny pack and leave the burnt-sienna couch that smells like cats for someone else.

PART THREE
Chapter Five

Who Gets (stuck with) the House?

"I'm goin' through the big-d and don't mean Dallas
I can't believe what the judge had to tell us,
I got the Jeep, she got the
Two bedroom, mortgage is due siding light blue palace"

Back in the good ol' days not so many moons ago, the biggest asset at stake in many divorces was the family home. The financial equity, sense of stability, and emotional attachment made ending up with the house after the divorce a very attractive prospect for each spouse. Fast forward a few years to the current housing market and it seems like the majority of divorces I handle involve a home that is underwater or close to it. It also seems that with many people losing their jobs or only working part-time, neither party is able to take on mortgage payments on their own after the divorce goes through. The fight has often changed from who gets the house to who gets stuck with the house.

In the past, home owning couples going through the divorce process had a lot of good options on the table for dealing with the family home. One spouse could buy out the other spouse and remain in the home, then refinance the loan to remove the other party's name. The couple could agree to sell the family home and split the profit. The couple could even agree for one person to keep the home and give their ex a lien for the equity in the property.[24] For the lucky few who still have any

---

24 The lien (which is kind of like a loan with collateral) is recorded in the property records and has to be paid to the lien-holder spouse at some point, or at a minimum, when the house is sold.

equity in their home, these options (and more) are still on the table. The million dollar question remains: Who ends up in the house?

There are some obvious advantages to walking away with the house in a divorce situation. From a financial standpoint, you don't have to worry about making a new down payment, qualifying for a new home loan, covering the cost of moving, or any of the other expense that come with relocating. You also know exactly what you're getting with your current home and can avoid the risks of finding a new one, like surprise repairs, difficult neighbors, or hauntings from the ghost of a long-ago tenant. From an emotional standpoint the sense of stability, especially if children are involved, may be a reason enough for someone to want to stay in a home. On the opposite end of the spectrum, I do run into a lot of situations where a party doesn't want the house because they'd rather make a clean start, which is perfectly understandable as well. You can remove the furniture and paint the walls, but even the world's most powerful Pantone can't erase bad memories.

The options for couples that have negative equity in their home are a little different. Selling the home outright is often a no-go because both sides would have to come to the closing table with bundles of cash in hand. Having one party keep the home is sometimes not ideal either since the party that's awarded the home often will no longer qualify for a refinance, which leaves the other party stuck with their name on a mortgage indefinitely. And of course, the potential negative consequences of short sales and foreclosure are well documented.

Even worse, the negative equity in a home isn't generally taken into consideration on the balance sheet we talked about last chapter during the division of debts and assets. Common sense dictates that if one party takes on a house that's worth

$200,000 with a $300,000 mortgage, it would be like taking on a $100,000 credit card debt, right? Not so. Homes that are "upside-down" are usually treated as a break-even or neutral asset when dividing assets—in other words, a zero on the balance sheet. The reasoning behind this I most often hear is that the person taking the house gets the benefits described above (stability, not having to move, etc.), and the housing market is expected to rebound at some point, so it would be unfair to count a theoretical negative equity since the house isn't being sold right now anyway.

Now that I'm done spouting all the doom and gloom I can about home ownership, there are actually a few good methods to deal with upside-down real estate. If neither party wants to live in the home permanently, foreclosure is sometimes not a bad option. One party gets the benefit of living in the house for free during the foreclosure process—which the other party should get some compensation for—and both parties walk away free of the house. The downside, of course, is that credit scores and tax returns usually take a hit in the process.[25]

If one party does want to stay in the house, a clever attorney can arrange this in ways that minimize the consequences to the other party. If the spouse staying in the home can refinance, great – problem solved! If the spouse staying can't refinance the mortgage, it gets a little more difficult. Just like with credit cards, the mortgage company doesn't care that a divorce decree orders one party to be responsible for a jointly held mortgage. If one party falls behind on payments, guess who the bank comes after for the money? It's also difficult for the person who moves out to qualify for a new mortgage

---

25 Note – If you are thinking about going through a foreclosure PLEASE speak with an experienced real-estate attorney first. There are ways to do it right, and there are ways to do it very, very wrong. I've seen experienced Realtors do it the very wrong way in the past, resulting in tax losses to their clients in the tens of thousands of dollar range.

when they're still technically responsible for the old one. One common solution is to put a time limit on how long the person keeping the house has to refinance (say three years) and hope their financial situation and the housing market improve by then. If a refinance still isn't possible, the house can be placed on the market for sale, or the person keeping the home can agree to make good-faith efforts to refinance every year after that.

Finally, what happens when nobody can agree on anything and it's left up to the court to decide? As I hope you've learned by now, there's no way to know for sure what's going to happen in that case. It all depends on the judge, the individual circumstances, and a multitude of other factors. Many judges will routinely order houses to be sold and the proceeds (or deficiency) split equally. Some judges will try to keep the house with whichever party is the primary custodian of the children to maintain stability in their lives. And other judges change their minds from day to day, flitting about like little robe-clad butterflies on a gust of wind.

The final decision as to who gets, or who gets stuck with, the home is such a toughie because it involves financial, emotional, and practical considerations. It's definitely one that works out best if the divorcing couple are on the same page about their goals moving forward, and take a realistic approach to who can afford the house and how to get the other person off the mortgage loan. The irony of the old country song lyric that started this chapter is that the complaining singer probably drew the long stick on that deal if it was done today – especially if the Jeep was Barbie's hot pink.

PART THREE
Chapter Six

Bad Behavior

Given all of the lovely things we've talked about so far, what I'm about to say next might be hard for you to believe. Sometimes during a divorce emotions run high and people behave badly. In my practice I've witnessed so much nastiness between two people who used to love each other that I almost don't trust my eyes. I go into every divorce hoping the couple will be able to be somewhat reasonable and amicable, but unfortunately that just isn't always the case. In Minnesota, we have two main methods for addressing unacceptable behavior, a domestic abuse Order For Protection (OFP) and a Harassment Restraining Order (HRO).

It is important to know that both an OFP and a HRO are filed independent of your divorce file, and they often won't be heard by the same judge that has been assigned to your divorce case. OFPs and HRO's are both available to anyone, not just divorcing couples, but they are especially common at the beginning of the divorce process. Each one has serious consequences if violated, including potential jail time, loss of eligibility for certain professional licenses, and loss of the right to carry a firearm.

Orders for Protection are granted when one spouse commits an act of domestic abuse against the other spouse. Without getting too technical, domestic abuse means that physical pain has been inflicted, or a serious threat of or intentional attempt to inflict physical pain has been made. OFP's can also be brought on behalf of a couple's children if they're alleged to have been victims of domestic abuse. As part of an OFP, the court can make a determination of who gets to live in the couple's house, what the temporary custody and parenting time should be, and set child support and other financial terms between the parties.

Harassment Restraining Orders are a bit less powerful than OFP's but still not something you want used against you. They are most commonly granted when one party repeatedly harasses the other, and the other person is adversely affected by the harassment. Things like stalking, showing up at public events to harass, making continued unwanted phone calls, and "targeted residential picketing" will lead to the issuance of an HRO.[26] Unlike with an OFP, the court probably won't decide issues about custody or child support. What they will decide, however, is who gets to stay in the residence and what limitations on contact between the parties should be ordered.

OFPs and HROs are a completely necessary, though unfortunate, part of the law. When one spouse reacts to the admittedly frustrating divorce process with violence or harassment, there has to be a way for the law to make it stop. The criminal and civil penalties and cessation of contact that come along with the issuance of a HRO or OFP are pretty powerful incentives to calm the situation down a notch or two.

However, another thing that can cause me to check my prescription is that both of these measures, OFP's in particular, can be abused by a less than scrupulous spouse or opposing attorney. Everyone who doesn't already know will quickly find out that the court process usually moves along at a glacial pace. Sometimes an attorney or self-represented party will bring an OFP motion because they want a quick route to get their custody and child support matters in front of a judge, even if there are no incidents of domestic violence. Often times, even the threat of having an OFP issued against them is enough to make a party agree to an unfavorable parenting time schedule. It's a dirty little trick, but one that I've seen happen many, many times in my

---

26 Hey, it's in the statute – see Minn. Stat. 609.748 for a full definition of what constitutes "harassment."

practice. I truly wish there was some sort of punishment (other than bad karma) for being the boy who cried wolf in this situation, as it both causes an unfair fight and muddies the water for those people who legitimately need an OFP or HRO.

This is another part of the divorce process when it's absolutely critical to have an attorney by your side. The civil, collateral, and criminal consequences of having an HRO or OFP issued against you are long lasting and serious. Conversely, if you are the victim of harassment or domestic abuse, you really need an experienced attorney to make sure you're protected from further incidents. Honestly, this is the one chapter of this book that I wish nobody ever had to read – but if you do and it hits home, get in contact with an attorney right away to talk about the specifics of your situation.

What other kind of financial help do you need when divorcing?

By Terryl Johnson, CDFA

Since the financial outcome of any divorce has such a great impact on the financial future of the parties involved, doesn't it make sense to get help from a specialist? Using a Certified Divorce Financial Analyst (CDFA) will increase the chances that a settlement will be reached that both you and your spouse can live with. It is only human to fear the unknown and especially at the beginning of the divorce process the financial fears of each party are heightened. Each is likely struggling to figure out how they are going to get through this financial crisis.

It certainly doesn't help that you have to make serious financial decisions while your emotions are changing by the moment. Adding to the stress is the immense pressure on you to get everything right the first time, since there are no do-overs. This is just another reason that a Divorce Financial Specialist can be so helpful to you, to be the voice of reason when it is otherwise hard to hear.

A CDFA will help point out details that may otherwise be missed between parties and even attorneys. For example, not all assets are created equal, since different assets can be taxed differently or not at all. For example one dollar of IRA money is not the same as one dollar in a savings account. The dollar in the IRA when withdrawn will be taxable at ordinary income tax rates, so it effectively may be only worth $.70, where as the dollar when withdrawn from savings account will have no tax consequences. A CDFA does projections to confirm that a proposed settlement is fair to both parties.

How a CDFA helped one couple:

John and Jane are 40 years old and have two children. They own a home worth $165,000 with net equity of $77,500. Their IRAs and 401(k) retirement plan total $165,500 in value.

John earns $90,000 a year and has take-home pay of $68,760 a year. Jane has never worked outside the home and has no marketable job skills, but she hopes to get a part time job for $8 an hour with take-home pay of $8,900 a year. The following settlement has been suggested: After the divorce, Jane and the children will keep the house. She will also receive $44,000 of the retirement moneys and John $121,500, thus dividing the assets equally. John will pay Jane spousal maintenance of $600 per month for 5 years and child support of $225 per month per child. He will also pay college costs which start in 4 years. John's expenses include his normal living expenses, child support, spousal maintenance and college costs. Jane's expenses include support of the children and are reduced when each child leaves home. This appears to be a reasonably fair settlement. However, an analysis creates the financial future illustrated in the following graph. Jane's assets will be completely depleted within seven years while John's investments will grow dramatically.

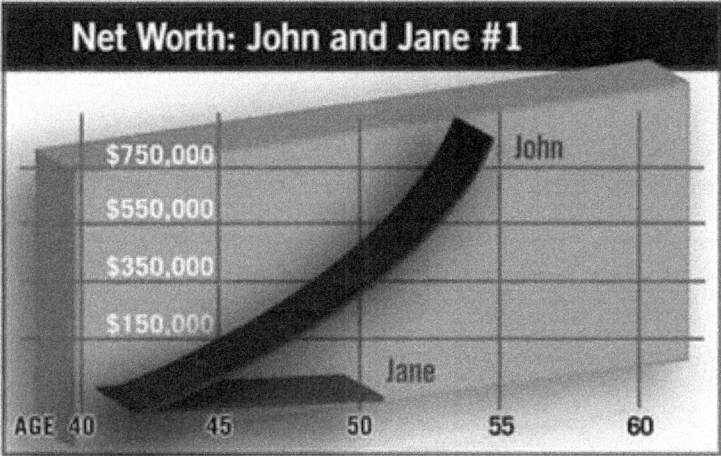

Net Worth: John and Jane #1

To improve Jane's financial future, the settlement could provide her with increased spousal maintenance of $1,500 per month for 10 years. This would actually cost John $1,005 per month in after-tax dollars. The correct child support according to the Child Support Guidelines is $1,125 per month for two children for a couple with their income. Jane also could be awarded an additional $24,300 from the retirement plans. She also may need to cut her expenses by 10%. These changes in the original settlement will produce the results illustrated in graph #2. John will still have a surplus which he can add to his investments. If John stays within his budget and invests all of his extra income, his investments have the capacity to grow to $2.5 million by the time he is age 60.

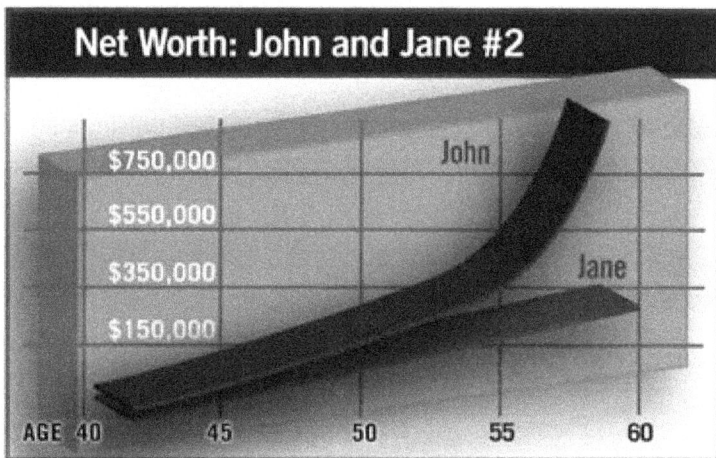

Net Worth: John and Jane #2

This sample case illustrates the value of financial planning as a means of reaching more equitable divorce settlements.

TOP FIVE ITEMS TO CONSIDER WHEN BEGINNING THE DIVORCE PROCESS:
  •   **Your new budget** - Often when we think of the word "budget" we think of it as a negative term. When you are in

the divorce process, knowing what your necessary expenses are is key in negotiating a reasonable settlement. Using a Certified Divorce Financial Analyst to help fine-tune your budget and project cash flow provides you with an understanding of what you need not only in the immediate future but in the long term as well.

- **Managing your credit** – Obtaining a copy of your credit report is essential to expose all joint accounts and accounts that you don't use or may not know about.
- **Dividing the "stuff"** – Make a short list of the items you want and the ones you must have. You may not get everything so be prepared to compromise when negotiating.
- **All assets are not created equal** – Different accounts and assets you may own have different tax consequences. Enlisting the help of a CDFA will ensure that you don't suffer any unintended tax consequences and that the division of funds is truly fair and equitable.
- **Not considering the long term impact of settlement options** – Many times what looks fair at first glance may in fact be totally skewed when analyzed and projected out for the next 10 or 20 years.

Terryl Johnson is a Certified Divorce Financial Analyst and a Mediator

After a successful career as a Financial Advisor for almost 30 years, I no longer give investment advice or manage money. I started Divorce Financial Directions to not have any "conflict of interest" when helping my clients analyze proposals and decisions presented during the divorce process. My clients have found that having knowledge and support can help take the guess work and emotionalism out of making decisions at a time when making logical decisions matters most. I have a passion for helping people. I can act as a consulting advocate for one party or as a neutral/mediator for both. I am on the MN Supreme Court Rule 114 Neutrals Roster and a member of the Cooperative Practice Network of Minnesota, serving on the Executive Committee.

Helping Your Children Through a Divorce

By Nicole Schwarz, MA, LMFT, Parent Coach

As a therapist, I've worked with many children while their parents were in the process of getting a divorce or after the divorce was finalized. Parents are often surprised by some common themes I hear from children in therapy.

- Most children wish their parents were back together. No matter how old your child is or how difficult life was prior to the divorce, most children wish their parents were married again. It may seem irrational and unreasonable to you, but remember, your child's reality has been the two of you together – for better or worse. Rather than fight this instinct, empathize with your child, and then move the conversation back to how life is now or how it will be in the future. *"I know you wish daddy and I could live together again, and even though that is not going to happen, I'm so happy to spend some one-on-one time with you!"*

- Your child loves you both. You may be severely upset with your former spouse, but more than likely, your child still loves you both. It may not be easy, or it may feel unfair, but children need to hear that it is ok to love both parents. *"You love your mom and dad very much!"*

- Can parents' divorce their children? Many children have a fear that their parents will divorce them, especially if they do something wrong or bad. Remind your child that parents do not divorce kids, emphasize that you will be their parents forever; nothing they do or say will change that fact.

- Some children feel responsible for their parent's divorce. Remind your child that they did not cause the divorce and that their behavior cannot influence the outcome of the judge's decision.

How to Support Your Child

Divorce is such a life changing event for families; parents are often unsure how to help their children. Here are some suggestions for helping your child through this transition.

This is a HUGE change for your child, even if there is less arguing or if it is less stressful in the home. Each child will work through it in their own way. Some children will want to talk about it; some will need more reassurance, while others will avoid any mention of the topic.

Children grieve and process feelings differently than adults. While adults tend to talk through a problem or stuff it away, children grieve and process in "bubbles." That is, they may be extremely sad, upset or angry for a short period of time, and then return to playing contently. Do not force the child to continue to process their feelings, allow them to move on until they are ready to talk about it again later.

Children may also process feelings of anger, resentment, worry or sadness through behaviors such as tantrums, arguments, aggression or non-compliance. Think of this as seeing their feelings coming out "sideways." Children do not always have the words or vocabulary to express what they are feeling, so instead they demonstrate it through actions.

Listen openly, without judging or giving your opinion. It may be difficult to hear what your child has to say, but your reaction to their disclosure is very important. If you respond by staying calm, not getting defensive or angry, your child will learn that it is safe to talk with you.

Resist the urge to "fix the problem" or state your side of the story. Instead, listen quietly until they are done talking and paraphrase what you hear them say. *"So it sounds like you really enjoy going fishing with dad and his buddies."*

- If your child is upset, search for a feeling word to use with your paraphrase. *"It sounds like you were*

pretty worried when mom was late to pick you up."
- If your child is expressing a concern, encourage them to brainstorm options, rather than offering your solution. *"What would make you feel comfortable in your new room?"*

Allow your child to feel and express a variety of feelings. They may express love for both parents or feel mad at one parent; they may feel sad, angry, confused, resentful, upset, relieved, grieving, or unsure about future. You don't have to agree or understand; just let them know it is ok and that you are there to listen. Respect your child's opinion about their other parent, and resist the temptation to join in with your own comments. Help your child find their voice to express their concern to the other parent. *"Do you want to write dad a letter to tell him how you feel?"*

Wait to introduce a new significant other until the relationship is serious or committed. When you introduce a significant other, both parents can emphasize the fact that it is ok to love mommy, daddy and the new significant other; and it's ok if they don't love the significant other right away. Continue to have one-on-one time with your child and be open to hearing any questions or concerns they may have.

Watch for signs that your child may be struggling with the divorce. If you observe major changes in your child's sleeping, eating, bedwetting, isolation, nightmares, drop in grades, socialization, or aggression, it may be helpful to talk with a mental health professional. You may also want to look into divorce support groups through your child's school or community center. Don't assume your child is fine or unaffected by this life change. Talk with your child often and be willing to listen when they are ready to talk.

Transition Day – Welcoming Your Child Back to Your Home

Regardless of your parenting time schedule, your child will need time to adjust and settle back in to their new environment. Here are a few tips for managing this transition time.

- Make exchanges civil. Do not engage in negative interactions, arguments or bring up past hurts during drop off or pick up. If needed, keep your conversation to a minimum and leave as soon as possible.
- Keep the conversation light and positive. Rather than drilling your child about the time with their other parent, allow your child to talk about whatever is on their mind. Sometimes it may be unrelated; sometimes they may share something about their time with the other parent. Your neutral but "willing to listen" attitude will help your child feel comfortable talking about concerns in the future.
- Allow extra time for your child to transition home. You may want to keep expectations to a minimum for a few hours or plan a simple routine that you do each time the child is dropped off.
- Do what you can to make going back and forth between houses easy for your child. Have toys, books, and clothes at each house. Create a checklist to remind children what to bring on transition day (stuffed animal, blanket, soccer cleats, backpack, etc.).

Working Together

Most parents' say that they want to put their child first, they want what's best for their son or daughter and would do "anything" to help. That is, until the other parent starts dating, buys the child an expensive gift or lets the child go to a sleepover on a school night. Here are some tips for working together.

- Keep communication civil. Regardless of your method of communication – phone, text, email – if you are communicating with your former spouse in anger, your children may be able to sense the tension and frustration. If you must have a heated discussion, plan a time when the children are out of the house.

- It is OK to express your feelings, however, limit the details you share and resist the urge to confide in your children. Own your own feelings, but keep it general, *"I'm feeling frustrated right now."*

- Agree to focus on your house and your parenting decisions, rather than criticizing the other parent. Statements such as, *"this is the rule in our house"* or *"that was your dad's decision"* may help you stay neutral.

- Focus more on having a strong relationship with your children rather than out-doing the other parent. Remember, your child loves you both. There is no need to "buy" your child's love or criticize the other parent.

- Remain united, if possible. One of the best gifts you can give your child is to remain consistent and unified even after the divorce is finalized. Even if you cannot see eye to eye on parenting philosophy, agree to speak respectfully about the other parent in front of your child.

- Limit the amount of information your child has to share between parents. Use a notebook that is exchanged at drop-offs; agree to text an update prior to transition days or use an online calendar such as Our Family Wizard to stay up to date on appointments or schedule changes.

- Allow your child to communicate with the other parent when they are in your care. Again, your child loves and needs both parents. Give them privacy while on the phone; resist the urge to pry into other parent's life, use your child as a messenger or yell things while child is on the phone.

- Respect your child's right to privacy in therapy. If your child is expressing concerns or feelings about the divorce in therapy, think of this as a step towards health, rather than a threat to your parenting time. Therapists are not parenting time evaluators; their job is to help your child process feelings and emotions. Therapy is also not an avenue to get details on your former spouse's behaviors or activities.

- Divorce is hard for adults too. If you are struggling, find a friend, support group or therapist to provide support. If you have concerns related to your former spouse, talk to your lawyer, a mediator or parenting evaluator.

Nicole Schwarz is a Licensed Marriage and Family Therapist.

Nicole is the owner of Imperfect Families, LLC and has been working with children and families for nine years, first in Saint Paul, Minnesota, and now in Saint Louis, Missouri. Nicole has a therapeutic practice focused on strengthening families and helping children, especially those ten years old and younger. Nicole believes in the power of positive parenting, and employs a cognitive-behavioral approach to therapy. You can learn more about Nicole's approach at www.imperfectfamilies.com.

You Need Support

By Bruce Smith

It's is not rocket science, divorce is gut wrenching. Even further, it is an identity crisis on steroids. Think about it for a minute. Marriage vows launch your new identity when the minister says "I now pronounce you husband and wife." From that moment foreword you start to create an identity as a couple. Unfortunately, when divorce occurs, every aspect of the "couple" identity that was built will change:

- Your role as a partner – gone
- Financial situation – split
- Parent – from full time to part time or even no time
- Friends – many begin to take sides or choose to wait and see until they re-enter your life

People deal with change and emotional stress differently; some like to share and talk, others are more introspective and may journal. Regardless of how you deal with it, releasing that negative emotional energy is like creating a big hole in a dam. It's a freeing feeling and it makes you feel better. Perhaps at first, only for a moment - but over time, moments turn to minutes, and minutes to months, and so on.

That's why support is so important; it is an outlet for your emotional release. While in the throes of divorce and even after divorce, it is important to create your own support network or find a support group. Having this emotional release is only the beginning of the benefits of your support network - there are so many more reasons to seek support, including:

- a place to make and build friendships
- a sense of belonging and camaraderie
- a forum to exchange ideas

- support to keep you on the right path and moving forward
- an environment to support your life changes
- a glimpse into your future situation
- a place to vent or talk openly and honestly
- a way to give back to people
- a reason to get you out of the house

One member of our support group even found a job through our group that resulted in a nice pay increase. So the benefits go far beyond emotional and social benefits. Before you go out and join just any group, here are a few pieces of advice to consider when looking for a support group:

> *What to Expect In a Support Group* - A support group should "feel right" to you. There are many different types of support groups, from faith-based groups to topic specific groups (like anger management, co-parenting, etc). Whichever you choose, it should feel right when you attend.

> *When to Consider a Support Group* - As the founder of a national support group organization, I recommend finding a support group as soon as you feel you need one. Don't wait. One of the primary benefits is knowing you're not alone. There is a true sense of relief when you are going through something with others. A big secondary benefit is learning from the experiences of others. This helps you prepare much earlier and be successful with your divorce.

> *Is a Support Group Right For You?* It's not a matter if a support group is right for you, rather it's the size and the topic of the group. For all the reasons I've already listed, a support group can benefit anyone, it's more about determining if the group fits with your personal preferences. For example, If you don't like big groups, then find a smaller group or start a smaller group of your

own.

How to Find a Support Group? We are lucky to have the technology we do. Finding a support group is only a few clicks away, just visit your old friend Google and complete an internet search. However, sometimes support groups are not internet search visible, so a few other resources to consider include:

- Lawyers
- Therapists or psychologists
- Friends and family (especially those that have gone through divorce)
- Meetup.com (internet social networking group)
- Religious leader/church
- Community centers
- Financial advisors / CPAs

What Makes a Good Support Group? When you visit a support group natural questions are – Is it a good group? Will it fulfill my needs? Will it be helpful? The best way to answer these questions is to take action:

- Call or email a group organizer. How long   does it take for them to return your call? If he/she does call back, share what you're looking for and ask if that group will fulfill your needs. Ask what other services that group provides to see if they offer services beyond what you were thinking.
- Research the group. Go on the internet and see if the group has a website and read about the group to see if it is a good fit for you
- Go to the group. I'd suggest going at least twice to get a good feeling. Then, listen to your gut.

When you attend, how organized is the meeting leader? Is the information provided is a professional manner? Is it useful information? Is the group well run? If the answers to these questions are "yes". Then you've found a great support group.

Bruce Smith is not an attorney or therapist, but is an integral part of the divorce community in Minnesota. Bruce is a divorce strategist coach and founder of The Divorced Guys and The National Divorce Men's Network. Bruce is passionate about the power of support; knowing "you are not alone" in the divorce process lightens the emotional load and can be empowering. Bruce draws from his experience as an author, group leader, speaker, divorce coach and his personal divorce experience. For more information, visit www.thedivorcedguys.com.

Navigating Through the Bankruptcy Process

By Jacqueline Kuiper, Attorney at Law

So...you're divorced and in debt. Sounds like fun, right? It may be time to file for Personal Bankruptcy. Don't worry – the process is not as painful and intimidating as it sounds.

An individual or a married couple generally files for bankruptcy in order to obtain one or more of the following benefits:

- To have certain debts discharged completely or sort out which debts are dischargeable from those debts which will still be owed;
- To receive extra time to pay debts;
- To receive a break from creditor calls while debt relief is arranged; or
- To have professional assistance to pursue lawsuits or other claims so that the money obtained can be used to pay creditors.

A discharge is a court order that forgives a debtor of certain specific debts. The discharge order prohibits a creditor from attempting to collect a debt that would otherwise be owed. However, not all debts are dischargeable. Parties can file written requests called adversary complaints to have the court determine if a debt is dischargeable. Typically, you can discharge all or most of your unsecured debts (like your credit cards, your unsecured loans, and your medical bills). Some unsecured debts are not dischargeable – typical examples of debts that can't usually be discharged are:

- spousal and child support obligations;
- certain tax debts;
- most educational loans;
- debts related to injuries or death caused by

103

driving while intoxicated; and

•   debts arising from fraudulent conduct.

This means that if you qualify for bankruptcy, you can discharge most of your unsecured obligations, but you still may need to pay your taxes, you have to pay your student loans, and you still have to pay your child support and/or spousal maintenance that you just worked out in the divorce proceeding. Debts that are secured by real estate or personal property are not dischargeable. For example, a creditor may be able to seize property even after a discharge is granted because the debtor has not kept up with payments. Even though the creditor may not collect on the unsecured portion of the debt, the property can still be foreclosed upon or repossessed.

Of course, there are negative consequences of filing for bankruptcy, and in some situations they may outweigh the benefits. For example, a potential debtor may need to resolve one debt (such as a mortgage), but if the home does not have any equity, there may not be any benefit to filing for bankruptcy. There will be an impact on your credit history as well, but it may not always be as debilitating as you might think. It is always helpful to first consult with a bankruptcy attorney to learn how a bankruptcy may affect your specific financial situation before undertaking any steps to actually do so.

There are several types of personal bankruptcy proceedings, the most common of which for individuals being the "Chapter 7". This is a "liquidation" bankruptcy and can be used by an individual to obtain a discharge of many debts without making payments in the future. In this scenario, a trustee is appointed to take control of certain assets of the debtor (or assets that the debtor recently owned) and to sell or distribute these assets for the benefit of creditors.

There are generally two ways for individuals to qualify to file chapter 7 bankruptcy: By passing the "Means Test", or if the bulk of the debtor's debt is "business-related". This determination is pretty complicated , so it is important to do detailed research or meet with a bankruptcy attorney to see if your situation qualifies for Chapter 7 relief. If you do qualify, the entire Chapter 7 process starts with the filing of a petition, which contains a basic description of relevant information about the case, the debtor, and the attorney.

You are not required to have an attorney in order to file a bankruptcy petition, file other documents, or represent yourself at court hearings. However, it is difficult for an individual to be aware of and protect all rights without the assistance of a competent bankruptcy attorney. There are many forms to fill out, lots of important deadlines, and several notices that a debtor will receive from the court. Bad advice may be worse than waiting to file for bankruptcy as it may result in a bankruptcy case getting dismissed. A debtor does not get a refund if the bankruptcy case is dismissed, and a debtor may not even get the relief that was hoped for.

Immediately after a bankruptcy case is filed, an injunction (called the "Automatic Stay") is generally imposed against certain creditors who want to start or continue taking action against a debtor or the debtor's property. It is important to read relevant statutes from the Bankruptcy Code or to consult with a bankruptcy attorney about the Automatic Stay because in some situations there is no Automatic Stay at all, or there is only an Automatic Stay if the debtor obtains a court order. There are many different time frames and deadlines, and creditors (such as child support services) may still take action to collect from a debtor.

Next, a meeting is held so that creditors and the trustee can ask questions about the debtor's financial situation. The debtor is placed under oath, and must provide sworn testimony as to the accuracy of the debtor's schedules. A debtor who is an individual must attend this meeting in person and may have an attorney present. If a debtor does not attend the meeting, the bankruptcy case may be dismissed.

In a chapter 7 bankruptcy case, all of the debtor's property belongs to the bankruptcy estate unless the court makes a ruling that certain property is no longer property of the estate, the trustee abandons property to the debtor, or the property is exempt under either federal or state law from collection by creditors. A "trustee" is appointed to take control of certain assets of the debtor, bring these assets into the estate, and sell or distribute these assets for the benefit of creditors. A trustee has the power to recover certain assets that were previously transferred and bring those assets into the bankruptcy estate.

An individual debtor can often choose to keep certain personal property (such as an automobile) by entering into a Reaffirmation Agreement. A Reaffirmation Agreement turns a debt that would be discharged into a debt that will not be discharged. This is a decision that should rarely be made and should only be done if the creditor is giving up something in exchange, such as a reduction in loan amount or interest. The Reaffirmation Agreement can be entered into after the bankruptcy case is filed, and there are very detailed and specific requirements which must be complied with.

In some cases, there is an additional step called the "Adversary Proceeding". An Adversary Proceeding is different from the main bankruptcy case - The main bankruptcy case involves a debtor and its creditors. An Adversary Proceeding in bankruptcy court has the same meaning as a lawsuit in other courts. This means that one or more "plaintiff(s)" file a "complaint" against one or more "defendant(s)." The most common forms of adversary proceedings are brought when a plaintiff requests that either a certain debt be excepted from discharge, or the debtor's discharge not be granted at all.

Regardless of whether there is an adversary proceeding

or not, an individual going through the bankruptcy process has obligations to complete. Typically, these include:

- Completion of courses in both credit counseling and financial management
- Keeping the court updated in changes in personal information, such as address or employment
- Read all mail sent by the court related to the bankruptcy case and meet all deadlines set by the court
- Attend the Mandatory 341(a) Meeting of Creditors
- Being honest!

The court currently charges $306.00 to accept the petition package. My professional case fee varies case-by-case. Factors that affect professional cost include case complexity, amount of debt and number of creditors affected, whether there's a need for significant asset-protection and exemption analysis, and consultation on potential adversary proceeding matters. Professional case fees can range anywhere from $1,500.00 in a straightforward case to $8,500.00 in a significantly complex case.

The earliest date that a discharge will be entered is shortly after the sixtieth (60th) day following the first date set for the meeting of creditors (described above). A trustee or the creditors have sixty days after the first date set for the meeting to file a complaint objecting to discharge.

If this is not a debtor's first bankruptcy case and the debtor received a discharge of any debts in a prior case within the last eight years, the debtor may not be entitled to a discharge in the current bankruptcy case. It depends upon the chapter number of the prior bankruptcy case, the chapter number of the current case, and the number of years that elapsed between the date that a prior case was filed and the date that the current case was filed. In other words: It's complicated and best left for an attorney to figure out.

For more information, I'd recommend starting with the resources below. Of course, I'm always happy to meet with people considering bankruptcy on an individual basis to provide more detailed information.

- www.mnb.uscourts.gov
- The Bankruptcy Code (11 U.S.C.)
- Federal Rules of Bankruptcy Procedure: http://www.law.cornell.edu/rules/frbp/
- Bankruptcy Forms: http://www.uscourts.gov/FormsAndFees/Forms/BankruptcyForms.aspx
- Bankruptcy Basics: http://www.uscourts.gov/FederalCourts/Bankruptcy/BankruptcyBasics.aspx
- Bankruptcy Basics (YouTube Video Series): http://www.youtube.com/user/cacbtv

Jacqueline Kuiper is a licensed bankruptcy attorney in Minnesota.

Jacqueline is a solo practitioner based out of Minneapolis Minnesota. Prior to owning her own firm, Jacqueline was an associate at a prominent Minneapolis bankruptcy firm for four years, and was also a bankruptcy trustee. She has experience working in the banking industry negotiating and drafting business contracts and was also an intern for the former Chief Judge of the United States Bankruptcy Court for the District of Minnesota. Jacqueline's legal practice focuses on representing and counseling individuals who are going through the chapter 7 bankruptcy process. She is always happy to answer any questions you may have about the process – feel free to contact her via email at info@kuiperlaw.com.

Divorce and the Homeowner – Working with a Mortgage Professional

By Mitch Irwin, loan officer

One of the most common, difficult, and emotional decisions made when going through a divorce is determining where each party will live afterward. The couple that formerly shared one home has to make several difficult decisions throughout the process that can have long lasting effects. Should the marital home be sold? Can one party afford to keep the house? Can the vacating spouse qualify to buy another home? This chapter will briefly touch on each area to hopefully make the decision a bit less complicated.

Selling the House

When the current home is too expensive for either party to keep, the home is usually sold. If there is equity, the parties usually split the proceeds and each party often uses their share of the proceeds as down payment on another home. In more recent times, there are a lot more homeowners who unfortunately owe more on their home than it is worth. If the home is "upside down" the parties may need to consider a short sale or foreclosure. Some realtors specialize in these transactions and can help explain the difference between the two. Both are considered a negative credit event that may have a financial liability owed to the creditor and a credit consequence that will determine when the borrower is eligible to buy another home. It's a good idea to meet with a mortgage broker or other professional who is experienced in this area to determine the potential benefits and impacts of a short sale or foreclosure, as it can be pretty complicated.

Keeping the House

If one party wishes to and can afford to keep the home,

doing so can be a good option, especially if kids are involved, as it can provide stability during a difficult time. [27] Keeping the home also eliminates the cost & stress of moving/finding a new home. Many times the person keeping the home will be asked to refinance the home into their own name. This releases the vacating spouse from the liability of the old loan and can provide access to the equity that is owed to the vacating spouse. Sometimes there are additional benefits like lowering the monthly payment (if the new loan has a lower interest rate or longer term, for example), or freeing up cash to pay off other debts.

It is always wise for the person keeping the home to consult with a mortgage professional early in the divorce process to determine if they will qualify for a new loan, what the timelines will be for closing the refinance and other important items to make the process trouble-free. This homework helps the client know what to expect for a housing payment after the divorce, and can also give time to take any necessary steps to come up with up-front costs or to clean up their credit if needed. It is important to note that despite what you may sometimes hear mortgage money is still available and interest rates have been low - however some of the qualification rules have changed.

An experienced loan officer knows how to navigate the mortgage rules in conjuncture with the legal timelines. The most common issues I see relate to:
1. Using child support or spousal maintenance to qualify
2. Timing: when to start the process, when to order the appraisal and when you can close.
3. Determining the difference between qualifying for a

---

27 Zach's note: however – be careful about locking yourself in to the thought that keeping the home gives a party the advantage in custody proceedings. Most judges see through this tactic pretty easily.

home loan and truly being able to afford the house. Use a budgeting worksheet to make sure you won't be "house poor."

4. Loan Structure: The ability to pay out equity to your spouse depends on several factors - how much equity is left in the home, how the decree is worded, and if there is a current second mortgage that needs to be included in the pay-off or subordinated. Each detail can make or break the ability to fulfill the divorce settlement.

5. Assignment of debt: knowing how to exclude the other party's car payment, credit card, etc.

6. Ensuring that the wording of the final divorce decree is written to optimize your financial position and won't present any stumbling block in the refinance or new home purchase process.

These are a couple of the major topics that can make or break a deal. There are a lot of other secondary topics that come into play as well; a good loan officer will help address these and set a plan for a smooth closing.

Buying a New Home

Once someone has owned a home, most people want to buy again instead of going back to renting. However, a divorce can complicate things if not done correctly. Much like refinancing an existing loan, careful attention is needed to make sure the post-divorce home buying process proceeds without difficulty. Partnering with an experienced loan officer during the divorce process can help you determine:

1. Timing: when can you write an offer on a new house and when can you close on that new home. I receive one call a week from someone panicking because they can't close on a house they made an offer to buy. Normally this is because they tried to buy a house too soon, before the divorce was complete. Most loan underwriters require

the final, signed divorce decree to determine:
   a. The exact dollar amount of any child support or alimony obligation.
   b. That the down payment money is yours and not joint funds.
   c. The old home is sold or awarded to your ex-spouse.

2. Support Payments: once obligated to pay child support, will you still qualify? How much can you afford? It is a good idea to experiment with the effect of a range of potential payments early in the process so you don't fall in love with a home that is out of your budget.
3. Down payment:
   a. How much is needed? Different loans require different minimum amounts. The most common options are FHA which requires a minimum down payment of 3.5% of the loan amount and has pretty flexible gifting options. Conventional loans require 5% which must come from your own funds.
   b. Where will it come from? The source of funds makes a huge difference as to when the money will be available. Gifts or "liquid" accounts like a checking/savings account are available almost immediately, but processing a QDRO[28] for your half of the ex's 401k can take several months. This is important to know before you make an offer on a home and set a closing date.

These are a couple of the big issues that come up when

---

28 QDRO refers to a "Qualified Domestic Relations Order", which his the court document used to divide funds held in certain retirement accounts. These can take quite a while to process, often several months before funds are actually available to spend.

dealing with housing issues during a divorce. The best piece of advice I can give you is to involve the lender early in the process and make sure they have experience dealing with these specific types of loans. Identifying the issues early and creating a game plan will take away a lot of the stress and eliminate last minute surprises.

Mitch Irwin is a loan officer with Bell Mortgage in the Twin Cities. He is a twelve year mortgage veteran, helping clients in divorce represents over 50% of his business. He welcomes the opportunity to answer your questions or to help with home purchase or refinance. He can be reached at: (612)210-3640 www.mitchirwin.biz | mirwin@bellbanks.com . (NMLS #451627| Equal Housing Lender)

About the Author

Zach Smith is a family law attorney in Minneapolis, Minnesota and is the owner of Vox Law. Zach focuses his practice on divorce, custody, support, and related issues, and has handled many cases in district court, as well as at the appellate level. Prior to forming Vox Law, Zach was an attorney with a small firm in Cambridge, Minnesota where he focused on family law, along with being the city prosecutor for a small nearby town. Zach attended college at the University of Minnesota and later William Mitchell College of Law in Saint Paul, only blocks from where he grew up. He remains an active alum, volunteering and mentoring regularly. Zach has been quoted in such publications as Smart Money Magazine and the Huffington Post, and is recognized as a leader in his field.

Zach prides himself as being approachable, knowledgeable, and down to earth, and feels that it is incredibly important for his clients to be able to relate to him on a human level, especially given the intensely personal nature of family law. He opened his practice because he saw a need for a law firm that was based around helping people work through their issues without all of the intimidation that goes with the stereotypical impersonal "stuffed-suit" attorney working in the tall building downtown. Zach's philosophy in his practice is to provide excellent service and accessibility to his clients while advocating for their needs in a strong yet respectful manner in and out of court.

Prior to becoming an attorney, Zach worked for years in the corporate world, first as an operations manager for small businesses in the 'burbs, and later in human resources for Supervalu, where he worked for over five years. More interestingly, Zach loves working on his home and in his shop on his fleet of not-quite-classic cars. Before going to college at the U of M, Zach attended tech school to learn auto repair, a skill which he still enjoys using whenever possible – except in the cold Minnesota winter. Zach lives with his wife and step-son in the Twin Cities area and is happy to talk cars, hockey, pinball, or indie music with whoever is willing to listen.

If, after reading this book, you or someone you know has any questions about a divorce, custody, or other family law related issue, please feel free to contact Zach. Vox Law's websites are http://www.vox-law.com and http://www.divorcecustodymn.com or feel free to email him at zsmith@vox-law.com. For those who prefer interacting with an actual human voice, Zach's phone number is 612-331-3449, and he's always more than happy to set up a free initial consultation at his office.